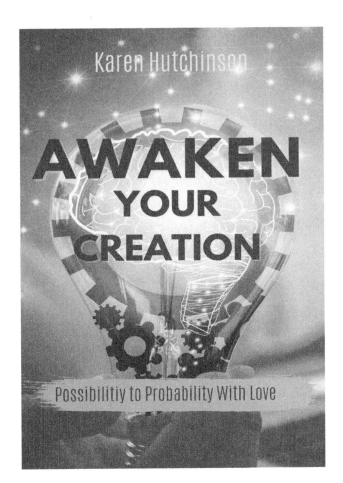

Karen Hutchinson

AWAKEN
YOUR
CREATION

Possibilitiy to Probability With Love

AWAKEN YOUR CREATION

First published by Hope View 2021
Written by Karen Hutchinson

Cover created by Karen Hutchinson

The right of Karen Hutchinson to be identified as the author of this work has been asserted by her in accordance with Copyright, Designs and Patents Act 1988
To find out more about the "Believe Releasing Process", Higher Self, Laws of the Universe visit www.5thdimensionearth.com

ISBN 978-1-8383982-0-0

AWAKEN YOUR CREATION

possibilities
to probabilities
WITH LOVE

AWAKEN YOUR CREATION

Contents

Karen Hutchinson ~ Founder and Creator of HOPE
VIEW
Love for Life Ignition Coach

INTRODUCTION

Hi Gorgeous ones, I'm Karen and welcome to Awaken
Your Creation.
A little bit about me and also how you can get best use
from this book and all it holds for you.

Ten years ago I started my journey of discovery towards
living my life on my terms. I took hold of my emotional
status and my responsibility of my life decisions and
made significant changes to start curating it, as I truly
desired.

Many of these changes were not taken lightly and were tough which at times caused disruption for my family and myself however there was something within me that just told me to keep going. This inner voice told me that my happiness was important too, not just the happiness of those around me.

I am a wife to Paul, and mother to Samuel (23) and Danielle (18) and my fur baby Dottie (2). Up until November 2020 I worked in the corporate world as a Retail Area Manager, looking after many retail stores with 100's of employees over the time span of 30 years.
Life was good, Life was busy, Life was demanding, Life was testing, Life was Life.
Some experiences affected me through my 49 years on Earth more than others did. Some were considered expected and others consequential, but all in all I felt I had done a good job.

However, things were not always as I would have liked them to be nor as they should be and as a result my Love for me deteriorated. It was a slow and gradual process. One that actually started far earlier than my conscious mind allowed me to realise. As when we have experiences that affect us emotionally we can be very good at suppressing the feelings and carrying on. Until one day you get to the point of full capacity and there is no longer any room for us to store them and something gives way. It will give way either mentally of physically.
Long story short my decisions and actions brought me to a place of Awakening.
A word that I originally thought was associated with people who sat around a campfire, holding hands, meditating and were completely out of touch with the real world. People who wore fluffy jumpers, and quite

frankly a little but weird. (Sorry guys, it was just my perception) I am sure I am not alone with this preconceived notion.

The Truth is Awakening is actually Living your Life consciously whole. Understanding why the emotions you have suppressed made you feel the way you do. It means allowing you the courage to choose Love emotions over Fear emotions. It means truly understanding them and then being able to fully let the go for good, so you are no longer impacted by their vibrations.

My journey of discovery of living life on my terms led me on a path of self-development. I worked with a couple of great coaches who helped me understand there was a better way of living my life. I started to really understand Law of Attraction and that the best part of my Life up to that point was because of my inherent Knowing about energy and how it works with our wondrous Universe.

A few years ago I met the wonderful Olivia & Raf Ocaña of 5th Dimension Earth who started sharing energy practices guided by their Non-Physical team. This understanding felt so true to me. I could feel my Knowing activate like it had radar attached to them. 2 years ago they shared the 'believe releasing process' at a retreat I was privilege to be a part of.

'Believe' is a God given process and the fastest way to Awaken on the Planet. Now before you start to think this is a religious book, let me stop you right now. It is not religious, nor will I refer to any religion. I will however refer to God. As God is the Creator of our Universe, regardless of whatever religion you follow or not. I told you no fluffy jumpers in sight. (No offence meant to fluffy jumper wearers)

Over the period of 18 months I completed my Awakening fully. It is important to understand that each step I took along the way started making an immediate impact on my Life for the better. Mentally and Physically.

I am now able to navigate Life in a much more Loving way. I am no longer impacted by the emotions of my past and I get to do Life each day at a much higher vibration. I get to Live Life with acceptance of who I am without fear of judgment. Do I have ridiculous days? Yes of course, I am human, but the difference now is I do not have to stay there for very long, sometimes not at all because I get to choose how I want to feel.

As a result I have navigated further Change in my Life with so much ease, from daily decisions to who I allow to influence my emotionally, to deciding what I want to eat. Most recently having the ability and understanding on how to navigate a couple of huge Life changing experiences.
COVID19 impacted everyone greatly in 2020, not just due to the illness itself but also lockdown and the knock on of everyday life too. I navigated the lockdown and community life changes really well however I did not escape this impact fully and as a result was faced with redundancy in November 2020. I had the courage to trust in myself to step away from all I have ever known and launch myself into a career I had a real Desire to do for a long time. I absolutely loved helping other people and supporting them through change and I felt as real nudge to share what I had learnt over the previous years about taking responsibility for your emotions and how you

allow them to impact your daily Life. I had a huge pull to support others with their mental wellbeing. In both my career and family and friendship communities I had witnessed the impact this grief had on so many and seeing them struggle to find their way out.

I stepped into the trust I held in myself to start guiding and supporting others and helping them to navigate their way back to 'Loving the Life they are Living' by Creating HOPE VIEW and becoming a full time Life Coach.

As a fully Awakened Soul I am always fully guided by my Non-Physical team who Love and support me. This enhances my ability to receive true guidance for my clients.

This is what changed my Life and it is what can change yours too.

I have been able to love myself fully through the Transition of my wonderful Dad who died of Cancer in September 2020, and if it were not for the emotional freedom I am now able to experience, this loss would have been even tougher to manage. I dedicate this book to him as he taught me lots about Creation in his own purposeful way, and I know he has been supporting me through the Creation of this book boosting my courage and confidence to start living an Extraordinary Life.

We are so happy to be sharing this wondrous process with you in a way that you get to decide how you start your Awakening. You get to decide what you would like to do to activate this new wondrous way of creating.

Consciously Whole Creation is where I lead from now on as it has changed my life for the better and it is our Purpose and Intention to show you how you can do the same.

As you work your way through this book and its process you will find meditations, energetic practices and exercises to support you. You have full access to audio versions of these at www.hope-view.com/awakenyourcreation-book

There is also a Universal Download section at the end of each chapter for you to make notes of any, ahhh haaa moments, realisations, Truths understanding, ideas, or any thing at all for that matter. I find it so useful for me to be able to make notes in the book I am learning from so I was guided to do the same for you.

WHAT IF

What if you could do anything you desired without any limitations?
What would you do?
What would you want to create?
Where would you want to go?
What would you do there?
What would you want to see change for you, for your family, for others or for this planet?

Maybe your desired change is something personal to you, for you. It could be an aspiration in your career, a physical change, to achieve an expectation or challenge you have set. Start your own business, invent a new concept, change of career, or even relocate to a new country, the list is endless.

Maybe your Desires are on a scale of global impact. Inventing the next energy efficient generator, a new way to recycle plastic, designing the most efficient mode of transport or the next big app to support mental wellbeing. All these Desires come from the same energy stream of possibility. Change comes from the energy of transformation and Creation. The new ideas come from the energy of Curiosity.

All of this flows from deep in your Soul and then heads on a journey of discovery. A discovery of your knowing, of your understanding, of you allowing and you igniting what you need to remember to do, as you have been destined to do all of these things and so much more. This is why you even have awesome Desires in the first place.

Humans are born with a huge part of their Soul ready for Creation. Having a Desire in your mind and on paper is one form of energy.
Really feeling the Desire within your Soul and what it would feel like in the having of it generates a totally different energy and therefore, the probability of a totally different outcome. Your energy influences the outcomes of all that you do.

You get to decide its scale of magnificence. You get to decide how much you push for this Creations success. You get to decide how you curate your life and the outcomes you Desire to experience. I get it though, there is always something that just keeps you from the success you Desire, or the results you want to achieve. Sometimes this prevention is totally obvious to you and other times you just cannot quite put your finger on it.

You agreed to come to Earth to co-create with God to expand your Soul, to expand the planet and to expand the Universe. All you need to do is remember How and Why. What is it you agreed to create within your Soul contract? Why is it you are consistently pulled towards a particular topic/skill/trade in your life that you feel you want to make a difference to or with.

The understanding that I share with you will allow enlightenment to Flow to you.

Let's get back to what has been stopping you?

Fear!!

The sneaky emotions that always prevent us from stepping into our awesomeness and allowing us to co-create Magic.
Fears such as lack of knowledge, lack of acceptance, lack of worth, lack of direction, lack of support, lack of self-belief, lack of funds, lack of ability, etc. etc. etc.

Your energy and your low vibration have potentially been holding you back from even getting started. Or it has been a stop start process on many occasions. Perhaps have you found yourself getting off to a great start but then the energy fizzles out, your conscious thoughts get in the way, somebody says something that throws you off course and before you know it you have given up. Or you have put out to the world a Creation that holds no love, lack lustre energy, no desire for change and a low vibration intention.

You may have been successful in the Creation process but failed to see the success you felt it deserved or the timing of it all was not great due to other external influences that is going on around you.

The impact and pace to which this has affected you of course depends upon the level of low energy and low vibration you are holding within you.
This vibration can be held at a conscious level, sub conscious or even unconscious level within your mind.
This vibration influences your thoughts and beliefs.
Beliefs you hold about yourself, beliefs about others

opinions of what you are doing or Desire to do and beliefs in what you think is possible or not for you. It all ultimately affects your energy and frequency to attract the most positive outcome you deserve.
Does this feel all too familiar?

I feel you! I have felt all of the above. I have felt the frustration of wanting change, needing change, desiring change in many aspects of my life for so long. Yet some of these aspects were a real struggle to get there at a pace or even at all. That is until now.

The Truth is, you just were not ready to receive the desired outcome just yet. This is because these previous attempts were all part of where you are today or there were just too many dependencies preventing your success. This all forms part of your future successful outcomes and this time you will be in a much better vibrational state of being with so much more understanding for the journey to really feel the benefits that all this success will bring your way. Just feel the truth in that, all of this perceived failure was all by perfect design. It all happened for you for your understanding, expansion and readiness to be ready for your path of Wonder, Joy and Fun.

Now I know how to do all of this and really step into my destiny here on Earth. I am really excited to share leading edge insight on how this works and how you too can implement this change process into your life.

It is my purpose to Illuminate Possibilities for all. To connect you back to feeling the most amazing energy of Love and Hope. It is my purpose to show you how these powerful energies together with a coating of magic; real

magic will 'Awaken Your Creation' energy and so much more.
It is by perfect design for you to create your own awakening journey through the power of Creation itself. This is such an awesome way to move through your life path and connecting to your light path at a quicker pace. Awakening whilst following a passion of yours and achieving success.

It is important to say right at the start, not all changes we Desire are going to be felt by all. They will however be felt by you and this is THE most important part of this understanding. YOU are the Creator of your Creations.

If your Desire is to start a new fitness regime to change your physicality, health and wellbeing or it is to build a multi million pound business, all will require the same amount of focused change energy although there may be some differences in terms of the amount of time or amount of action each Desire takes to unfold. No Desire is more important than another. No Desire is greater than another. Each and every single Desire is needed for the expansion of you and this planet. So, do not think for one minute that this book is not for you.

Every single human's Desires are important. You are important and have important Creations to manifest. All by perfect design and all in alignment with Soul contracts and pre manifested outcomes. Of course you all have Free Will and of course you get to choose how this pre manifestation will materialise. You will have full autonomy over how and when you do things.

Just know though that now you will be consciously receiving some awesome guidance along the way.

Universal guidance, so why would you not allow this guidance to flow with you throughout each part of the journey and beyond. You have already acknowledged that you have not had as much success as you would have liked previously completely doing it your way, right?

A Desire to make the bed will generate Creation energy. A Desire to grow plants generates Creation energy. A Desire to make a cup of tea generates Creation energy.
Understand that Creation comes in all shapes and sizes, yet all equally important for expansion of all in that moment of time. So even the perceived smallest of tasks in the process will hold equal amount of importance.
That said I am sure you are not reading this book with the Desire to learn how to make a decent cuppa now are you.

You have this book in your possession because you asked for it, either consciously or unconsciously. You put out to the Universe the request for guidance and understanding to help you move forward with your Desires.
Your Higher Self led you to this book because you already unconsciously know how to achieve all you Desire. You just need to Remember.

This book holds the energy of true transformation. It will connect you to the Truth of who you are. It will align you to the Desires that light up your Soul.
Just stop and feel within for a moment. Take a slow deep breath. Can you feel the energy of Hope already starting to activate within you.
You can feel this energy start to activate within your solar plexus. It is energy of excitement, it is energy of Hope, it is energy of change, and it is energy of limitless possibilities. This is your energy it is now waking up.

This is the energy that will continue to grow within your Soul. Feel into it at anytime you feel you need a boost of Hope.

This is not just another self-help book that may or may not help you. Absolutely not, you are far too important to this planet and I am equally as important to not waste my time-sharing regurgitated information.
You are important. You are needed. You agreed to co-create. You will make a difference to yourself first and foremost and to others should it be the right time for you to do so and for them to receive it. You are here to live a wondrous life, living it fully aligned to your Soul purpose.

It is time now for you to allow yourself to fully connect with all that this lifetime wants to offer you. This is your one and only lifetime here on Earth. You only get one shot at living a physical life and this is it. If you are struggling to feel that energy within you just yet, do not worry as this will start to grow throughout this process. We will shake up your energy and get it moving in a rhythm that flows and of a much higher vibration.

When I say we, I do mean "We" in a capacity of Universal influence. Earlier when I mentioned that you had asked for this book, this support, this guidance, it is because you already had a Knowing that there is a resource to help you. Consciously or unconsciously you already had a Knowing you wanted change. You may refer to your Knowing as, intuition, gut feeling or a nudge from the Universe. I will be referring to your Knowing as the ability you have which is strengthened as your conscious connection with your Higher Self is remembered.

Your incredible precious Higher Self is your truest connection with the Universe. He or she is always with you and they have been with you since before you incarnated on the Earth. They are your source energy, they are your understanding of all that you are, have been and Desire to be. They ignite the Truth of you for you to align to. They love you unconditionally and they are your biggest cheerleader. When you become a Conscious Creator you become a creator of true and loving energy sharing the highest of vibration you can be in each moment of Creation. So my friends, this is the first piece of magic for you to connect to and understand. You are always going to be more successful in all you do when are doing it consciously whole and from a place of Love.

There is a caveat to this understanding and there is no getting away with it. To create at the most highest vibration in all you do, say and feel you will be required to release low stored vibration. What I mean by this is that there maybe some specific elements of your life's journey so far that will keep you from moving forward fully at pace until you fully re-label these Fears to Love and raise your vibration. You will feel this and will receive guidance on this from your Higher Self of course, as they know exactly what you will need to do.

The energetic process and understanding that I will share with you throughout this book will indeed take you further than you have ever been before and it will also create success for you beyond. It will make a significant positive impact on your day-to-day living. Just know that now, there may be a nudge to side step into the releasing process more deeply throughout the process, depending on what it is you discover is holding you back and what you Desire to create.

If you are already awakened and fully love labelled, than this will be a different understanding for you, as this process will stretch you beyond your current perspectives. Therefore some new truths will be required to support a new perspective and understanding, but you guys are already pros in this part of the process and you will find the exercises along the way really helpful to keep you on track. Your focus will be to live your Truths.
Be excited though gorgeous one, as each and every one of you are on a journey to more Wonder, more Hope and so much more Love.

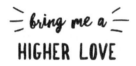

bring me a
HIGHER LOVE

Your first step to becoming a Conscious Creator starts here.
This is a beautiful meditation practice to allow you to practice connecting with your Higher Self.
Be in a comfortable and quiet space.
Close your eyes and focus on your breath for a couple of minutes
Allow your mind and body to settle and feel your blood flow almost come to a comfortable halt.
All you feel is the gentle rise and fall of your breath.
Set the intention to connect with your Higher Self.
Their energy will flow to yours through your conscious gateway at the top of your head.
Ask your Higher Self to flow their energy with yours.

Allow some time to relax with this connection and feel
your self soothe with their support.
You will feel their loving energy flow through your Love
vortex (chest area) and ignite the connection with your
loving energy. Share your loving energy back to them to
strengthen this connection together.
There is no rush with this practice.
Ask your Higher Self to connect you to the Law of Balance.
Allow this soothing energy to settle within your Mind,
Body and Soul.
Set the intention now with your Higher Self to allow
change to flow to you.
To allow the change in your understanding
To allow a change in understanding to work in a new way
To allow the change from what your Creation will bring
for you.
You do not need to know at this stage how this change
will come for you.
Just know that the perfect change is making its way to
you.
Stay in this connection for as long as it feels good for you.

Be excited!!

AWAKEN YOUR CREATION

≥UNIVERSE DOWNLOAD≤

UNIVERSE DOWNLOAD

AWAKEN YOUR HEART

You are now already on the way to achieving a completely different outcome for your Creation just by taking the step forward to re-connect with your wonderful Higher Self.
If this concept is brand new for you, I will share now just a brief understanding.
There is much more information to be found at 5thdimensionearth.com

Your Higher Self is your connection to the Universe. They connect with you through your conscious gateway at the top of your head through the penal gland. If you are male, your Higher Self is male, if you are female then your Higher Self is female. Throughout this process you may also receive their name too. So be open to the guidance and insight that comes your way. It is wondrous, exciting and enlightening. Your Higher Self has been with you always, ever since before you physically incarnated on this planet. They love you unconditionally and know you better than anyone else, even you. They have felt all your high vibrational experiences and of course have felt your low vibrational experiences too.
They are a totally high vibrational loving entity and share pure love with you always.

They will not energetically drain you, as their energy is totally aligned to yours.

I have wonderful connection practices that you have access to as many times as you Desire for the connections that I share within this book at www.hope-view.com/awakenyourcreation-book

When you truly awaken your heart to this wonderful connection you will be allowing a wonderful energetic flow from the Universe also.

Imagine having your own direct link to all the Universe holds.

Imagine being able to get answers to so many questions you may have about your life experiences. Well it is all about to start now.

Imagine how powerful your Creation and life in general will be with this incredible conscious connection and energetic flow running through it always.

When you awaken your heart to finding more Love and Hope to flow through it, it will ignite Magic within your Soul. This is Magic that every single human being on the planet has available, yet we do not allow ourselves the possibility of igniting it. Now that is a heck of a lot of unutilised Magic don't you think?

My darling ones, this relationship is truly magical, it will open up your perception to all you have experienced and continue to experience. It will open up the possibilities of what your life could look like moving forward. Your precious Higher Self will help you take the right opportunities that come your way to guide you on your light path and connect to all the pre manifestations you asked for and already have been given. These future manifestations are just waiting for your energy to align to them and this conscious connection speeds up this process.

Those of you who have already consciously connected with your Higher Self, you know the incredible support they have brought you. Now it is time for you to really put this connection into Creation. It is your time to step forward and align to your Soul Contract and create the magic that you asked to do before you were incarnated. This process will of course stretch you and for sure will bring up some wonderful new truths for you to create, but oh my the expansion to your Soul energy will be awesome. I can feel the possibilities for each and every person reading this book. I can feel the energy from you all as you connect to this understanding.

I have seen the potential impact this book will have on your life should you chose to allow it. My incredible Higher Self Sarah has shown me things that I would never have ever imagined for myself in this life time, yet every single time she shows me something new, it totally resonates and feels true for me. Many of these possibilities have manifested already, and I have so many more to come. This and so much more my darling creator is the wonder that beholds for you too.

I feel you, I see you I am with you in every word, chapter and exercise.
Our energy is here with you always. You can ask your Higher Self to connect with us and feel us cheering you on. When you hit the tricky moments, feel our energy supporting you. When you achieve an outcome at each stage of the process feel our energy Celebrate with you. This is the intention that Sarah, my incredible Non

Physical team and myself set before we even started writing this book.

This book is important. You are important. God asked us to create this guidance for you. We all have work to do to create Magic and Wonder for all. We are here to expand our Soul whilst on this wonderful planet and co-create for the expansion of all. This book is just the beginning but it is the important step of opening up this energy for you.

Remember the questions I asked in the previous chapter about What If?
Did you answer them from a place of Love and Hope?
Did you answer them from a place of Balance?
Did you even really give yourself time to answer them fully?

Even if you did answer these questions, do so again but now with this new understanding.
Do so from a place of Love and Hope.
Do so within a conscious connection with your Higher Self.
Now see what answers flow to you.
Now feel the energy that is within your Soul.
Capture all of this understanding after you have fully received it and once you feel you have received all you can at this stage. You will receive a confirmation from your Higher Self that they have shared with you all that you need to know right now, but do ask them questions for any further clarification of what you have received.

I have a Knowing this understanding felt so much more powerful for you this time round.

I have a Knowing you could feel this excited energy running through your inner being.

You have felt an energy within your Love vortex (chest area) you have felt and energy within your Hope vortex (solar plexus). If you did not feel it just yet do not worry, you will have a Knowing, or visions of what it is you are here to do.

You can carry out this exercise as many times as you feel you need to but start to Trust what you receive. Your Higher Self is excited to share this understanding with you.

⸛ BELIEVE ⸛

There is now an opportunity to set some Truths with your Higher Self at this stage. As there will be a few thoughts running through your mind of doubt and fear. This is totally normal. This is absolutely as it should be, as you are here to make a change within. You are here to start living and creating with new energy. You are here to Awaken and let go of low vibration.

Follow this connection exercise to start the Truth process off.

Sit in a space where you are comfortable and not disturbed.
Take in a nice deep breath and feel your body relax and settle

Bring your attention to your inner being and just feel as to where your Soul is. (between your solar plexus and your pelvis, the lower part of your inner being)
Set the intention to light up your Soul energy and feel this ignite.
Ask your Higher Self to come closer to you.
Feel their loving energy flow through your Love vortex, and share back your loving energy to them.
See this loving exchange of energy flow and allow your physical body and mind to relax.
Allow your mind to just slow down and focus on your breathing.
Ask your Higher Self to connect you to the Law of Balance. Feel this soothing energy flow from the top of your head all the way throughout your body.
Take a few steady breaths and feel this energy settle within your Mind, Body and Soul.
Now ask your Higher Self to connect you to the Law of Truth, feel this ignite within your Truth vortex (tummy area under tummy button)
State the following Truths.
The Truth is I allow myself to build this wonderful relationship with my Higher Self.
The Truth is I allow myself to trust the guidance I receive from my Higher Self.
The Truth is I allow myself to feel excited about what it is I am here to do.
The Truth is I am ready to allow the possibilities to flow to create something new for me
The Truth is I am excited to create a positive impact for myself
The Truth is I Desire to create something wonderful to support others.
The Truth is I am looking forward to feeling good throughout this process.

The Truth is I am ready to allow positive change to flow through me.
The Truth is I Desire to feel the importance of my Creations.
The Truth is I Allow myself to feel the trust in my creations.
The Truth is I Desire to trust myself to complete this Creation.
The Truth is I Trust my Higher Self will support me throughout my journey.
The Truth is I am ready to expand my Knowing and connection with the Universe.
The Truth is I Desire this experience to be fun whilst I am creating.
The Truth is I allow myself to connect to all the possibilities that will flow my way.
The Truth is I am ready to co-create with the Universe.

Allow yourself as much time that feels good to you in this connection to set any other truths your Higher Self is guiding you to make.
Do not worry if you do not get anymore, or feel you have missed any out. There is plenty of opportunity to capture them moving forward now that you are consciously aware that you can do so. These truths are really powerful when you can really connect to them and feel them resonate in your Truth vortex.

I have a very strong cognitive receiving capability. I have a strong Knowing. I have had this all my life, but I just did not realise it was due to Sarah's capabilities too. I have an amazing capability to receive unconscious thought from others. I receive understanding that they do not even know themselves. There are many other capabilities that I have enacted also. I am not sharing this to blow my trumpet, although it is pretty awesome ha ha. I am sharing because I used to believe that these capabilities where just for the chosen, the special ones, not for someone like me. Yet deep down I always hoped it would be something I was able to do. I always wanted to connect to Non-Physical and receive my own guidance and now I do.

In May 2020 I became one of the first Believe Accredited Practitioners for 5th Dimension Earth which means I leverage the energy of their incredible collective, The Abraham & Jesus Collective, this also means I cannot mistranslate for my clients. I went from hoping I could have a connection to Non-Physical to receiving full Universe downloads to help my family, my clients and myself all within 18 months.

We all want super powers right? The Truth is each and every single human has capabilities just waiting to be opened up. Your Higher Self is so excited to help you enact these capabilities. The only thing between you and these capabilities is your vibration, your understanding, your acceptance and your conscious connection with your Higher Self.

I receive beautiful messages and understanding from Sarah and other guides in many ways, one of the most Creative forms has been in the format of poems. This did take me a little bit by surprise, as this was such a new realisation for me. I share a few of these poems with you

throughout the book. They are special, they will be felt, and they will trigger a Knowing from your Soul too.
We Hope you enjoy them.

Awakening Your Heart

Awakening Your Heart
Is now your life's work
Supporting others Hopes
To live a life of Freedom

Connect to their Higher Self
For understanding is key
To unlock the emotions
To set the soul free

Go inside their minds
Deep in the sub conscious
That you don't see
And feel the connection
For the new truths to be

The trip cycle of emotions
That keeps them run ragged
Will heal so much quicker
When rewired and not jagged

Support them to set Truths
Understand the Believe way
And open the door for them
To living happier always

~ Karen & Sarah ~
April 2020

⸜UNIVERSE DOWNLOAD⸝

AWAKEN YOUR CREATION

UNIVERSE DOWNLOAD

THE HAMSTER WHEEL KEEPS ON TURNING

You have tried many, many times to change aspects of your life, change behaviours, change feelings, change actions, change relationships, change careers, but the change has either not shown up or has not lasted for very long.

You now Desire change you can see, change you can feel, change you already have a knowing of and change you can actually experience long term and feel elated in the having of it. You are not alone in this feeling. There are hundreds of thousands humans on this planet right now, in the exact same position.

I too was one. I used to believe that I was not worthy of my Desires. I did not deserve these changes I had written down in my journal. The Desires I had put onto my dream board, as for sure they were just dreams after all. It was a nice fluffy self-help thing to do. Now, don't get me wrong, vision boards are awesome, providing you are actually able to feel the Desire energy to go with them.

I had so many Desires on my vision board that had been on there for far too long. There were others that did manifest in a timely manner. These manifested Desires were what I considered nice to have and I didn't have to muster up some real energy to achieve them. I felt aligned to them and therefore I had the expectation that I would get them.

These manifestations were mainly about "Things" material things that I could see, feel and touch if I wanted to. These things already existed so I felt the truth of them. The things that I really Desire were emotional changes. I want to feel differently every day. I want to see the world. I want to work for myself. The problem was I did not believe in myself to be able to do it. My energy had become so dependant upon my day job to give me the things I desired. Yet it was my day job I no longer desired. Oh my, this hamster wheel went on for years.

I would try so many new possible business ideas, but they never really took off for me. Not in the capacity I needed them to in terms of receiving enough income to leave my well-paid career. I loved each and every one of these ideas, for a short while, and then the fun fizzled out and I started to get frustrated with the lack of promised outcome. I would more than likely find an excuse to stop it, as there was no reason for me to succeed.

I held the belief I am not able to achieve them because I was not special enough to have all I wanted in my life. I was here on the planet to live an ordinary life.
By ordinary I mean, only accepting what my life was offering in that moment. Being fear-full of wanting more, being scared to go for my dreams in case of failure.

It wasn't that I Desired more stuff really, a better car, a bigger TV etc. For me these things I connected to

manifesting. Plus to be honest I could buy them if I really wanted to. These were not my most Desired Desires.
I Desire to feel different within; I wanted to live my life in control of how I feel and how I react to situations on a daily basis. I wanted to try activities that I never even thought I would do. I Desired to do things I could only ever dream of doing. I wanted to write a book that would help people. I wanted to make an impact. I wanted change.

I wanted to do a different job; I was not connecting with my 30 Year career any longer, it didn't make me feel good. To be fair, I had done my time with that job, it was good to me and I was good to it; it was time for a change. I Desire to do something that made my heart sing every day. I Desire a job I could do to help other people feel good. Most of all I want to make a difference. I want to work for myself, in any location I chose to be in.

DESIRES

I want to raise the vibration of this planet. I want to make an impact. I want to leave behind a legacy of Hope for others to connect to. I want to be a change maker.
I want to know what it really feels like to live my life on my terms at the same time creating a wonderful understanding for others to do the same. Oh my so many things I want to do. I made a start and got stuck each time.

I could not quite find the courage to do all these things I desired.

There were many emotions holding me back. Trip cycles and behaviour disruptors are all linked to our low vibration experiences. To truly make a change with these repeated thought cycles and disruptive behaviours then you will need to embrace an awakening journey.

Awakening was my escape from all the low vibrations I was holding onto which in turn were holding me back. In this book I will take you through aspects of this wonderful releasing process. My Desire for all of you reading this book is that you use it to make a start at raising your vibration. Use the book to start making focused changes that you Desire to work on first. To allow you to scale up or scale down the process depending upon where you are on your awakening journey. Most of all my purpose for this book is to enable as many humans on the planet to become a Creator. I have a Desire for every human to become a Creator of their own Destiny, in whatever capacity that is for them.

The truth is I wanted to do all these wonderful things yet I could not find a way to get there. Yes, some things started to change, which was awesome, but it all still was what I perceived at the time to be "Too slow" and you know what happens when you don't get results…. You stop trying. Then you see other people jumping forwards, doing all the things you Desire and some more.

Why is it everyone else gets the break and not me I would think, sob and feel sorry for myself many times?
I am hard working.
I am a good person.

I am always here to support others.
What I was not was ALL IN. I was not all in for myself and
therefore I was not all in for my Desires. Most of all I was
not consciously connected with my Higher Self. My
wonderful Higher Self was the biggest missing piece of
the jigsaw.

All of these beliefs and emotions I held triggered my trip
cycles of lack of trust, lack of hope, lack of self-belief, lack
of worth, lack of self love etc. etc. These triggers worked
hand in hand with the disruptors.
It was time to get off the hamster wheel, make some
decisions and make a start for real change.

EMOTIONAL FREEDOM

Now I am living this one and only life that I have,
connecting to my precious Higher Self, who is always
illuminating my possibilities of true change and I am
going to show you how to do it too. This process will
enable change. Just remember though, it takes action to
create change. Not a wing and a prayer and leaving it up
to the Universe. You are the Universe my darling. Your
Higher Self is your direct link to all the Universe holds for
you. This means you hold all the possibilities for the
change to manifest for you. Now it is time for you to bring
these possibilities towards probabilities and create the
changes YOU Desire.

40

Are you ready to jump off the hamster wheel?

In this next exercise, connect to the change you want to make right now and ask yourself the following question. Do this exercise consciously connected to your Higher Self.

What is holding me back from starting this change?

Who is holding me back from achieving this change?

How would I Desire to feel to achieve this change?

Good Morning Gorgeous

As you start your day ahead
Are you filled with a little dread
Do you hold on to the past
Or just think the worst instead

Its time now to stop the cycle of
Hanging onto your fears
And connect to the hope
You can wipe away your tears

It is ok to feel sad
It is ok to feel sorrow
But darling not for too long
Or you will miss out on tomorrow

Hope is always there for you
Without any conditions
Just start with one ray of sunshine
And the rest will follow to submission

~ Karen and Sarah ~
June 2020

⌇UNIVERSE DOWNLOAD⌇

AWAKEN YOUR CREATION

⸗ UNIVERSE DOWNLOAD ⸗

BEHAVIOR DISTRUPTORS

If you always do what you have always done, you will always get what you have always got!!
You most probably have heard this saying before.
You may have also heard same shizzel, different day. Yes politely edited, but you get my point.

Your habitual thoughts and actions become ingrained within your mind and body.
Your habitual behaviours are ingrained within your thoughts and actions. They become one with the cells in your body. This is your state of being in that moment. This brings about a continuous trip cycle of events that bring you to the same outcome. It takes a lot of self-discipline to overcome these habitual cycles.

It takes re-patterning. It takes change in itself to create a change. It can be really tough at times. It can also be so freeing too, because once you capture these cycles and understand them you will be able to let them go for good.

Lets take food for an example. You have decided to stop a certain food group on an eating plan. You really have to plan ahead with what you will eat instead; you have to remind yourself that you are not having the food group at this time. You have to engage with will power to prevent you from eating this food. You have numerous conversations with your self about the whole decision about its elimination. You then feel crap about the fact you cannot eat it, you then feel resentful, annoyed, frustrated and so on. Then you revert to eating the food you were avoiding and start the process all over again.

There are many other aspects that flow within this example, but for the purpose of this understanding I wanted you to understand what behaviour disruptors can be like. They throw you off track. They can make you believe you are not in control. They can remind you of past experiences that did not make you feel good. They can stop you in your tracks of progress and feel lack of worth and confidence.

When you are setting about creating any change within you or starting a project for change for yourself or others, you will be battling against many behaviour disruptors. This is a highly probable fact for all. It is part of human life and it is because there are always other options available to us or the consequences of not following our desire for change are not big enough for us to make the shift. Or it simply is just too hard to stay focused on our desired outcome. All of these distractions will be linked to a fear or perception of fear, depending upon where your vibration is. Either way you need to recognise what it is that is causing this disruption. Is it fear of failure, fear of success, fear of judgement, fear of not being good enough, fear of moving forward, fear of missing out, fear of change itself, fear of the unknown?

As I sit here writing this chapter I am feeling the pull to go and make a cuppa and put out the washing!
Why exactly? I am really excited about writing this book. I am really excited to help people find a way to create their

own conscious change. I do not fear doing so as I am already fully love labelled. Yet I was still being distracted.

I knuckled down and carried on and then another disruptor of self-talk. The dog needs a walk. Maybe I should take her for a walk now instead of later, she needs a walk, it is my job to take her so I may as well just pop out now and do it. I need to do it sooner or later so I guess I should just do it now. This self-talk battle in my head went on for a short while until I noticed what was actually happening and I could change the energy of it all.

For me it was an unconscious perception disruptor. Do people even want to read my book; do they want to know about what I have come to understand through my awakening, do they even need it? Also there was a disruptor about how long it would take me to even write it. Do I have enough time? I have never even written a book before why do it now? I noticed the disruptive patterns.

This moment of distraction allowed me to ask for guidance from my wonderful Higher Self. I was able to make a plan on when I would work on my book and how long I would dedicate to it each day. I know I am not used to sitting still for such a period of time, so I allowed myself to decide what felt good. From then on I did not feel restricted to keeping my head down and cracking on with it. I mixed up the timings across the week and ensured I dedicated the right time of day for me for when I felt in full flow with receiving the insight for it.

I am receiving the insight for all of this as we go along. This is part of what I wanted to create in terms of understanding how we can consciously co create with the

Universe. More specifically with my Higher Self and my team of Non-Physical guides.

All of these avoidance tactics where disrupting my flow of writing this chapter for the very purpose of me being able to share with you what can and will happen for all. It is part of being human. It is connected to vibration. It is connected to previous experiences held in our conscious and sub-conscious mind that you probably do not even know is there.

I was being reminded that this would for sure happen for you. It was a little strange for me to be honest as I am already fully love labelled. I have gone through my awakening and have re-labelled all of my experienced fears to love.

However, I am very much human and therefore can perceive fear if I allow myself too as I have new experiences such as this, writing a book. With my armour of tools under my belt I am able to easily navigate these perceptions so much quicker now. Phew!

This is what I Hope for you and it is absolutely possible for every single one of you to achieve this should you Desire to do so should it be part of your Soul Contract.

What I do know for sure is that as you are now in possession of this book you are destined to create something wonderful. This is part of your Soul contract and this Creation is pre- manifested and you can achieve it by tailoring your awakening process to enable this Creation to go ahead.

The understanding of disruptive behaviour is crucial, as it will most likely pop up its head again in a different capacity further along the process. I am not saying a walk with the dog was not a good idea at this time, as it quite possibly did help me when I came back to the chapter and flowed with the rest of it.

What I am saying though, it is important to notice when you are allowing certain behaviours to disrupt you and throw you off track. As they can and will sneak up on you and catch you out. It may throw you off track for hours, days, weeks or even months, but just know you can and absolutely should come back to it as soon as you are in full alignment with the energy you want to put into your wonderful Creation.

⊱ ENERGY CHANGES ⊰

There are no rules stating you only get one shot at this Creation. Like I have already said, Creation is part of who we are. It is part of our Soul energy. It is why we came to Earth. You are human and you are living a human experience. Energy changes and so can you. However do not wait for too long, otherwise the Universe may prompt someone else to discover your Creation and put it out to the world before you do anything with it. Not as a way of punishment, no, not at all. It is because the world needed that Creation sooner rather than later. So my darling, if you have an awesome idea that the world needs, crack on

49

and get it flowing with its Creation before you miss your opportunity.

Now that you are ready for these disruptors, also connect with the understanding that your Creation will only flow with you if you are in flow with the right energy. Energy changes frequently, a simple moment can change your outcome on what it is you are working on. This chapter may have gone in a different direction had I not stopped so soon and took Dottie out for her walk, but just know that if this happens, be prepared for the energy to shift and what you expected the out come to be in that moment will differ to the next time.

This is absolutely ok as long as you align yourself to this understanding. Then you can connect in with your Higher Self for further guidance and support. They will help you ramp up the energy again to continue with your Creation. You may even receive the guidance to start over, go in a different direction or indeed carry on as you were. When you feel into it you will of course receive the right guidance so make sure you ask the questions.

Awareness is crucial to allowing yourself to re-pattern them in the upcoming chapters. Plus they can become pretty annoying to; especially if you are in full flow and then BAM up they pop. When you are finding yourself not cracking on with the tasks in hand notice what you are being distracted by, what thoughts are you thinking, what emotions are coming up for you? Make a list and then ask your Higher Self to share some insight with you around them. Some emotions or memories may well be clear as day in your conscious awareness.

Maybe some memories are hidden and you cannot quite make the connection with the experience. Do not worry, your Higher Self will only bring to you what it is you are ready to understand. Being prepared is being for-armed and Knowing that you can change these disruptive fears to love by setting these truths and of course all the other truths that your Higher Self guides you on in relation to the memory.

Remember you cannot ever do too many of these so really allow the time to flow with what comes fully. It is important to always do this process from a place of Balance so you can feel the truth of the emotion and or experience.

⹂FEAR TO LOVE ⹁

Set the intention to connect to your Higher Self
Ask them to come closer to you now.
Allow their loving energy to flow with yours
Share your loving energy back to them and feel this wonderful exchange of energy flow through your inner being.
Set the intention with them to connect to the Law of Balance.
Feel this wonderful energy flow through your Mind, Body and Soul.
It is from this place of Balance you can ask your Higher Self to connect you to the Law of Truth.

51

Feel the activation of this Law in your tummy just below your tummy button.

Set the following truths.
The Truth is I allow myself to connect to the possibility of success.
The Truth is I allow myself to let go of the previous perceived failures.
The Truth is I Desire to let go of judgement from myself and from others.
The Truth is my Creation will be good enough for me and to share with others should they require it.
The Truth is I do not need to fear this change and I allow myself to feel its possibility.
The Truth is I allow myself to let go of the fear of the unknown.
The Truth is it is ok not to know what the outcome of my Creation will be at this stage.
The Truth is I am good enough to create this wonderful change for myself
The Truth is I deserve to feel the full benefit of this Creation
The Truth is I am able to create wonderful and much needed change for others.
The Truth is I Desire to feel worthy enough of this Creation for change.
The Truth is I am a born Creator and I am here to do good for all.

There will be some more specific truths for you to create with your Higher Self along this journey to co-create, and you will possibly connect to a few more disruptors along the way, so just know you can come back to this exercise as many times as you need to regardless at what stage you are at.

Isn't this just so reassuring to know. You can capture every disruptor and re-label it as soon as you notice it. Your Higher Self will of course be flagging these to you along the journey because they know the importance of this change for you and to the success of your Creation. It is also good to understand that some truths will resonate with you in an instant. Others may require a bit more understanding. So be patient with your self in this process.

Time Out for Love

Time now for Love
Time now for Care
Time now for everyone,
Everywhere

To connect to love and
Go deep down within
To rest, re-charge and
Re-connect to who you are
For a bit more than a min

There's enough for everyone
Look after the young and the old
As the only ones who are vulnerable
Are those who fear their true mould

You have amazing power within you
To align to all that you are
Allow yourself to believe
How freaking great you already are

Drop the judgement of others,
On how they react in fear
Focus on those around you
Who love and feel you dear

There is an abundance of love for everyone
Be it food, water or supplies
Lets focus on connection and
Coming together to save all our lives

~Karen & Sarah~
March 2020

≈ UNIVERSE DOWNLOAD ≈

⌟ UNIVERSE DOWNLOAD ⌞

LET GO – DROP OFF THE BACKPACK

It is time to say goodbye to old mechanics, old habits, and your old ways of working, old ways of creating that are not bringing you the results you Desire.
It is time to let go of the triggers and disruptors you have been holding on to. These no longer serve you in this new Creation energy.
There is no energetic space for what was, when you are connecting to what is and what if.

You are starting something new and exciting. You are required to step into this new energy of Creation with so much love for your journey. When you continue to drag aspects of our life that are connected to the past, that are connected to low vibration experiences, you cannot fully step forward into the energetic vibration that you Desire to be in right now. This defies energetic laws and therefore stops the full flow of your Creative energy. This also confuses your Soul connection. Your Soul is going in one direction but your mind is taking you backwards. This totally discombobulates you and your Soul, which throws you completely off track. Can you just feel the discombobulating energy in these words as I describe what happens to you energetically? I certainly can and even if you do not feel this on a conscious level, your Soul will be feeling is unconsciously. That is how powerful your energy is.

Discombobulated energy does not allow you to move forward fully and in Flow.

Imagine yourself right now happily creating your Creation and all of a sudden you are pulled backwards in time to a place where you felt low vibrational and unsuccessful. Sorry not sorry to bring you there, but feel now how important it is to really be able to let go of these emotions. They will hold you back always. You may get better at managing them, and better at wading through this energy but the truth is, they need to go for you to be able to step fully into the magnificent Creator that you are.

There will be times throughout this process that you discover fears that you will not be aware of until your Higher Self brings them to you. Just know when this happens it is because they know that you are now ready to let them go.
Your Higher Self knows that now is the time in your Soul contract to gain full understanding from this experience and you can then fully let go of these fear-based emotions.

This is why I previously mentioned that it is absolutely OK to keep connecting to Creation, as many times over as you need to but you absolutely must do it a new way with new energy. Otherwise you will keep getting the same result. If you are trying something over again and again it needs a new approach a new understanding for the Flow to come through. It needs to be created without old energy. Letting the old shizzel go fully, allows you to step into a higher vibrational version of you. The version of you that you have been aspiring to re-align to for so long, yet did not fully understand how to do so. The version of you who has gained new understanding and perspective of what you are about to embark upon.

The Truth of You is making its way to the fore front. It is igniting your Soul energy in a way that it has not been able to do before now. Your Soul energy will start to glow so much brighter causing a chain reaction within your inner being, your vibrational frequency will attract further matching vibrations aligned with your Creation and so on in perpetual motion. This will create a magical triangle of consistent powerful energy exchange between You, Your Higher Self and Your Creation.

This is easier said than done, for sure. I know this. I have been in your place right now. It is however such a crucial part of the process. It is one you really need to allow some time for. You deserve to feel this change within you. Your Creation deserves to receive the best vibration from you always. This is what I meant at the start about doing things differently. If you really allow yourself to fully engage with the releasing process you will experience change like never before.

Imagine this, you are planting a seed in a pot with the intention of Creation, but for some reason unknown to you consciously it does not grow.
You then reused the soil and the pot and you gave it some water. However your vibration at the time was really low. You are having a really tough time with other aspects of your life and this low energy is flowing through everything you are doing, saying and being. This low vibration energy you are sharing is not powerful enough to ignite life into this plant. You keep watering it daily, as you are going through the motions but you have not changed how you are feeling. The plant sprouts a couple

of shoots but within a few of days it dies off. How is it, the basics for this plant was all met; yet it did not grow to its full potential?

The environment was not right for the seedlings to grow fully. You checked the light, you checked the air, and you checked the water levels and all were correct. One thing that you did not check was you, the creator of this plant. You too are a crucial part of this plants environment; you are a part of its Creation and Transformation. Everything we do receives energy from us.

Would you take the new seeds and do the exact same process again without changing any of the elements involved? Would you have even considered your energy vibration impacting the outcome of your Creation?

It is so important to notice your vibration within this process. Notice how you are feeling about this change and Creation. Your vibration dictates what you attract towards you and how this then manifests into your outcome. Your Creation feels you on every level. You are so important to Creation and its positive outcome. You can receive guidance from your Higher Self at any stage of your Creation to understand how your energy is affecting your outcome. This is such an influential understanding for your manifestation of your Creation.

This understanding brings so much Hope for you and your Creation. This new way of living consciously whole will change absolutely every outcome you Desire in your life, not just this Creation you are working on at this time, but the next one and the next one. This understanding is the key to your success and to enable you to achieve all you agreed in your Soul contract in your one and only

61

shot at physical life. Why the heck not use all available resource to you?

Consider your Non-Physical team as unfiltered sources of information.
True energy, true information of the highest vibration always. The higher your vibration, the clearer the information you receive. When you are storing low vibration you will infiltrate what you receive and therefore not always receive the correct guidance. This is why the releasing process is so incredible for you and your Creation.

When I do any project work now I always have a team meeting with my selected guides for each project. They steer me in the right direction, they share with me the information and understanding. They are my biggest cheerleaders. They always unconditionally show love towards me and we always get to have fun along the way. I ask so many questions at times for clarity and that's OK. It was a truth I had to set in my awakening journey as for me asking questions was a sign of weakness. I had a belief that I should always be able to get all the answers the first time. This definitely is not the case and it is important to remember that they are learning to tune to you as you are to them. It is a two-way energetic exchange. If this belief is one that you are holding too, then create some new truths with your Higher Self so that you can head this one off at the pass.

Whilst you are at it, consider whether you need to set some truths in regards of receiving guidance from all Non-Physical guides too. It is not unusual for this to feel tricky for many people. Especially if this is a new concept for you or you hold a belief that only the gifted few are able to connect with Non-Physical humans.

How amazing is it to know that you are totally in control of all the things you do not just within your thoughts but in your energetic vibration too. Your soul energy will influence your mind to bring a higher vibrational thought pattern, which harnesses a full circle of Soul expansion. You will gain a deeper connection to the truth of who you are at a Soul level.

It is important to let go of low vibration emotions around your Creation. It is crucial for the expectation of success. You are not doing anyone or anything a dis-service by letting go of old habits, old understanding and old ways of working. Just because you know only this way of doing does not mean it is THE only way.
To be honest, if it is no longer working for you this is enough evidence that it is time for a change right?
It is time now for you to energetically open the doors of possibilities of creating in a brand new approach. You have absolutely nothing to loose by giving it a try. Nothing at all, but you have so much more to gain. There are so many humans currently achieving a much greater success in all they do since stepping into the 'believe releasing process' and it is so magical to be part of. As a 'Believe Accredited Practitioner' I have the privilege to work with clients on a daily basis to support them through their awakening with this wonderful process.

Is it simple? Yes totally. Is it easy? No not always and some parts of the journey are tougher than others, but my darling you will be so free emotionally once you have found your way through it.

Your Higher Self literally holds your hand the whole time. Your guides are your biggest cheerleaders and together we get to change our lives for the better. On the other side of this process is a life filled with so much Wonder Hope and possibilities and it feels like you are stepping into an energetic space of true Emotional Freedom.

⟩EMOTIONAL FREEDOM⟨

In this exercise set the intention to feel into your current vibration levels. Take notice of where you are storing this low vibration within your physical body. Your Higher Self will trigger this knowing for you.
On a conscious level, what do you already know you are ready to let go of?
The conscious emotions can be completed first with your Higher Self by following 'The Truth is' process.

What is being stored in your sub conscious mind that is holding you back? These are emotions or experiences that are not obvious to you at this time.
Your Higher Self will bring to you a memory or an experience that you have suppressed and therefore do not realise on a conscious level that it is affecting you.

Please do not worry, your Higher Self will only bring to you what they know you are ready to understand and re-label. This memory could be something that you did not realise was affecting you in this way, so be open to what comes to you and trust it is correct. It is with this understanding that you can now set new truths in order to let go to move on.

These emotions can feel differently to you on a day-by-day basis depending upon what is going on in your current life experiences, as this will affect your transitional vibration. So be sure to feel back into the past couple of weeks to get a true picture, or indeed do this exercise each time you set about the next stage of your creation. It is so good to let go of old energy at each stage so that you can be at the highest vibration possible for your Creation.

Make notes or keep a diary of emotions that may pop up whilst you are not consciously working of your Creation. At times these emotions will be heightened by your Higher Self when it may seem out of the blue, or at a time that feels unrelated to you on a conscious level. Trust me when I say, your Higher Self knows it is the perfect time. Notice these occasions, acknowledge them and then work on bringing your vibration back into Balance before you connect to the law of Truth to address them.

Ask your Higher Self to connect you to the Law of Balance at any time you feel it is necessary. This is the preferred emotional state of being before taking action with the releasing process.
Allow your Higher Self to bring through any memories or experiences that are attached to these emotions.
When you feel into each one allow yourself to feel compassion for you in every experience first and foremost. Even if this experience is not happening

directly to you, it has still affected you, so allow yourself to feel this understanding from your perspective too.

If this experience is because of your doing, your behaviour or your choices you have made also remember that this is ultimately not your fault, but it is your responsibility for how it continues to impact yourself and others.
Have compassion for how these experiences have impacted your Vibration within every cell in your body. Allow yourself to feel this within your inner being.
It is at this point with clarity and understanding as to how these experiences have affected you that you are now ready to connect in to the Law of Truth with your Higher Self and set some new truths around each experience.

You can state Truths such as

The Truth is it is not my fault
The Truth is I am ready to let go of what is holding me back from being successful with my new Creation.
The Truth is I am not responsible for what I can no longer control.
The Truth is I Desire to explore feeling the compassion for myself in this experience.
The Truth is I allow the possibility of having compassion for those who made me feel this way.

There definitely will be more specific truths that your Higher Self will bring to you based upon your specific experiences, so please do allow yourself some time to receive these from them. Go back to them at a new time if needed. You cannot get this wrong, so be assured you are going in the right direction for positive change within.

Once you have set all the truths that you can connect with set the intention to "Let Go" of each low vibration you are storing in relation to these experiences and emotions.

Does it feel good to know you can move forward without the weight of that low vibration backpack weighing you down?
Does it feel good knowing that change is waiting for you always?
Does it feel possible that your Creation can become probable?
Feels exciting doesn't it?
The energy of Hope is starting to Flow more freely for you now.

Can you feel the ignition of this energy within your solar plexus?

TO PROBABILITY

Time to Let Go and Be free

As I sit here still with the sun on my face
I feel the tension I hold run away with grace
Its soothing warmth fills me with joy
Its rush of heat allows me to deploy
The truth of me rises to the top
I'm here in this moment filled
With so much love it won't stop

Love for who I am now
Love for who I evolve to be
Love for each and every moment
I have endured through eternity
All I have come to learn
I no longer need to yearn
For what was before now
I can let go of and be free

~ Karen and Sarah ~
June 2020

≥UNIVERSE DOWNLOAD≤

≥ UNIVERSE DOWNLOAD ≤

DISSOLVE LIKE ALKA- SELTZER

Letting go of your low vibration experiences is the first step. Setting the intention for these vibrations to dissolve and move away is next.
This is a great part of the process to use your full imaginary conscious mind.

Closing your eyes for this is helpful but not totally necessary.
You will be doing this exercise following your truths. As you visualise these low vibrations detaching from your Mind, Body and Soul see them as energy moving away from you. See these vibrations dissolve into the ether, so that they do not come back to you. Strong truths that truly resonate with you and felt within the Truth vortex below your tummy button will help the certainty, however this visionary exercise is so powerful too.

Seeing these vibrations literally move as far away from you as you can possibly see and now watching them dissolve into the air away from you. Giving them so much space to move on into the ether. Allowing this energy to dissolve away from you completely is setting the intention for the low vibration kinetic energy to not Flow back to you.

This may sound a little woo but in actual fact well it is the Power of Energetics.
As mentioned in the last chapter, you have a huge influence over your vibration and when you set the intention to dissolve these low vibrations around these specific experiences you will be sure for them to not return providing you continue to follow the next steps of course. This is a part of the process that some people do not fully connect to yet it is so important to really feel the power of this.

This step followed by the next is the way you can be sure to let this low vibration go fully. Of course you may have to do this a few times based upon each emotion and experience you are connected to, as this will depend upon your life's journey levels to date. For some of you there may be some trip cycles that need specialist support from a practitioner and these will be brought to you by your Higher Self, but also know there are so many that you are enabled to do for yourself too. Do not hold back see these emotions dissolve upon the truth settings upon each step of the way.

There is a huge energy of intention from you by completing this part of the process. Sending this low vibration away from you with love and compassion for you always is powerful and Soul expanding.

Be mindful that further truths may arise for you at this stage to enable full letting go and dissolving, and that is all part of the process.

Feel the relief and satisfaction of your amazing efforts already getting to this stage. This is not a journey to be taken lightly. However this is a journey of discovery, understanding towards emotional freedom. Just know that you are being taken through the aspects of your vibration that are currently affecting your success for Creation. This is what I love about sharing this wonderful process in this way.

⋛ ENERGY OF INTENTION ⋚

You get to create something wonderful through the process. You will have something so special and needed to share at the end of it.
You will feel so good within yourself Mind, Body and Soul you will continue this process further that I know for sure. Even if it is in stages through the energy of Creation again just know that your journey was meant to be this way, and this is absolutely by perfect design.

There are some of you reading this book that are already fully love labelled. This process is equally helpful for perspective controls and a great way to change them for you as you continue to live a human experience you will endeavour new experiences that may generate new emotions that are within your transitional vibration. This also enhances your truths enabling you to manage these so that they do not settle and you are able to let go and dissolve at a much quicker pace. Calling upon all your truths you have already set with your wonderful Higher Self, which is allowing you to be living your truths fully.

Just because this chapter is a little shorter than others should not let you consider it is less important. For this really is not the case at all. It is very important if you want to no longer be triggered by these low vibration emotions regardless of whether they are transitional and in the moment or indeed stored within your emotional body.

Dissolve your Fears

Night turns to day
Dark turns to light

On every occasion
Even when there is a fight

When you think it is tough going
The situation you are in

Know that the light is waiting
For you to allow it back in

Bring your spirit into balance
Connect to Hope deep within

Then watch with wonder
As life unfolds joyfully
Connecting back for you to win

~ Karen and Sarah ~
March 2020

≥ UNIVERSE DOWNLOAD ≤

UNIVERSE DOWNLOAD

BALANCE ALLOWS CLARITY

When you allow true balance within your Mind, Body and Soul you will confidently feel the deeper connection to the truth of whom you are. Balance also enables you to feel the vortexes within your inner being much more clearly. This clarity allows you to understand what the emotions are connecting you to in terms of experiences and memories, as you will be able to feel and see more clearly than ever before. You need balance in your daily state of being.

This does not mean laid back on an armchair sleeping, or actually it may do for some. It means being able to feel content, calm, happy emotions that you feel run through your soul. It means allowing the moments of major highs settle back into balance without yearning for the high again immediately afterwards. Let's face it; consistent high energy can be exhausting at times. Equally it means that if you are experiencing really low vibration emotions that you are able to raise yourself back up to balance much more easily and quickly.
This is vibrational mastery at its finest and it is an aspect of your life you will get better and better at mastering the more you let go of the low stored vibration emotions within you. It is a state of being where you get to receive

the absolute best guidance from your Higher Self and Non-Physical team, as you will not mistranslate the guidance because you can feel the truth of it.

You get to make clear decisions from this place, as you will be able to feel the truth of your thoughts and feelings ready to make the right decision for you.
You are able to flow more freely through curveballs and diversions of your plans, as you will feel the truth of these situations without taking it personally.

It is an awesome state of being to aspire to master. It is where you get to receive guidance for change, development and Creation. It is where the clarity and understanding settles in all you have come to learn in your lifetime.
As mentioned previously it is where you need to be before you re-label your truths, as from this place of balance you will also get to feel the truth resonating within your Truth vortex.
Here are a few statements to reflect upon to understand your level of balance.
Do you find yourself starting your day from a place of balance or from a frantic energy?
If the answer is yes, then you have some understanding to flow to.
Did you go to sleep in a balanced energy?
Did you get a good night sleep?

Did you set the intention to wake up in a balanced state of being?
Do you allow yourself enough time to do what it is you need to do in the mornings?

If you are good in the mornings, at what point do you start to feel the energy that is about to throw you out of balance?
How, what or why does this happen?
Is it something or someone or a particular location that this happens with?
Once you start to feel out of balance what are the usual consequences for you?
How does this then disrupt your day thereafter?
Do you have tools in place to bring yourself back into alignment?
These questions are the perfect starting place to explore what is affecting your vibrational balance.

Take your time with these and maybe keep a diary to help you understand more over a few days. It really helps you get clarity of what really is affecting your balance.
There are some people who flip from high to low vibration in an instant, there are others who have more of a gradual change, either way understanding what is triggering it for you will allow you to understand the emotions and experiences that are affecting you.

Your Higher Self will bring these to you; they will highlight what they know you are ready to understand. They will bring these emotions and experiences to you which initially will trigger the emotions in that moment but once you acknowledge this and understand it you can ask them to bring you back into balance before you connect in with setting new truths to let go of these fears.

80

Follow the truth process in the previous chapters to start the re-labelling process. Your Higher Self will bring these truths to you.

There will be some of you who are reading this book that are fully love labelled, as you have already taken yourself through the believe releasing process and therefore no longer have fear based emotions within you, however you may find yourself struggling at times with balance. This is due to your perception of a situation or a person and therefore will trigger agitation within you, which can feel icky and uncomfortable. You too can ask yourself the above questions to understand any habitual thoughts or habits that you will need to address and ensure that you choose love in each and every moment so that you can find your way back into balance. You already fully understand the power of balance. Yet at times you forget to utilise it. Pressurised jobs, family situations, the hustle and bustle of life can impact our self-care too, which will enable an in-balance within your transitional vibration. Just because you are fully love labelled, does not mean you should forget the basics, as it is now your responsibility to keep your vibration high and yourselves in alignment of the truth of who you are.

Your Higher Self can connect you to the Law of Balance when you ask them. This is such a wonderful law to understand and allow. This law was taught by 5th Dimension Earth in their publication "believe".

My Higher Self Sarah holds a unique ability of amplifying Balance and Desire in equal measures which is so awesome for me to harness, as this state of being is what allows me to really enjoy the high vibration moments in my life where by I truly feel the happiness and Joy within my inner being to the core of my Soul. This also means that when the low vibration experiences come my way, I feel the truth of them so much quicker now and although I may feel the sadness and frustration of the situation, I am able to bounce back to balance in a flow of ease with the desire for change with love not fear.

It is important to remember that you are physical humans living a physical life, and therefore you will not be shielded from life's events and experiences either high or low, and that's ok, the difference is you no longer want to let the low vibration experience emotions store within your physical body.
I never ever go to bed with low vibration. I will do everything I can to release it from me. You know the saying "Do not go to sleep on an argument" Well this is why; you do not want to allow it to settle with in you. You want to be able to understand it, let it go and move on.

There are so many ways you can ignite balance within your inner being.
You can go out into nature and flow your energy with its energy. Notice how incredible nature is. When the strong winds hit nature it holds its ground. For example a tree will stand tall and proud. The braches and leaves may sway from side to side but its foundations are strong. The wind settles down and the tree just keeps on being true to itself and adjusts its elements within and then takes the necessary action to keep on growing and glowing. It does not hang back worrying if the weather will hit again or

what the other trees were thinking of it or whether or not it should keep on growing. No, it has its purpose and reason for being a tree. This realisation is just so inspiring.

Nature has so much to share with us about being the best version of ourselves. Nature inspires us to be part of a community. It inspires us to flow more with life. Nature inspires us to see that we all have seasons of change and possibility and sometimes there are challenges and potential set backs, but if with think and feel like a tree we will find our way back into alignment and balance in a much easier way with less resistance.

=̲ LOVE =̲

You can set the intention to connect your energy with nature and even be specific to connect with a tree, visualise and feel your energy flowing with the trees energy. Ask your Higher Self to amplify this connection for you so that you may feel the strength of this tree within your inner being. You can draw strength from nature to support you and fill your balance levels back up. Feel the calm and balance that this nature object is sharing with you. You are nature and therefore your energy can align with all nature energy.

Love and Hope ignite balance within your inner being and when you allow the energy to flow back into your inner being you will feel the balance settle with you. You can the direct this wonderful energy out to every cell within your body to re-pattern your energy flows.

Do this exercise with your Higher Self, as they will amplify this for you.
Feel their energy flow with yours and allow your souls energy to flow with theirs.
It is such a wonderful practice to enjoy at any time you choose. Even if you are having a good vibrational mastery day you can still ignite this wonderful energy to enjoy. Do it as you are going about your day, do it when out in nature, do it whilst in the supermarket. Do it as much as you can, as you can never get bored with feeling this good.

Your cells love it. You will feel the buzz with excitement. This is Self-Love for you. This energy ignites healing for you. Physical, emotional and spiritual healing will activate and start working together more freely.

HOPE

Balance is also found in your breath. You know when your breathing is out of alignment as its pace changes. When you ask your Higher Self to consciously help you connect to your breath, you will feel where in your body needs it. On each intake of breath you can guide where it is needs to go. You can feel it relax the part of your physical body you send it to. On each out breath you will feel the release of tension you are holding. You will feel a noticeable difference within your body and feel it start to come back into balance just with this simple technique.

It is from this wonderful place of balance that you get to make decisions about any situations that arise with a much more confidant expectation of the outcome you desire.

The more your Mind, Body and Soul are in alignment the more your Soul will expand, the better you will feel in your vibration and the better the outcome of your Creation will be.
For balance is the key to success. It allows you to Feel Love, Choose Love and Be Love more often than not.

Your Vibration is Your life's work

When all around you is a bit frantic
And life feels out of control
Connect to the Law of Balance
And you will be back on a roll

Curve balls in life are part of our Souls challenge
Understanding the lesson and letting go is for you to
manage

Mastering your stored vibration
Is now your life's work
To connect and let go of
Emotions that do not have worth

Love Hope Joy and Laughter
Are the vibes we want to embrace
So start your awakening journey with Determination
and Grace

~ Karen & Sarah ~
March 2020

UNIVERSE DOWNLOAD

⟩ UNIVERSE DOWNLOAD ⟨

CHOOSE LOVE

Whenever I hear or read the word 'Choose' I am immediately taken back to my teenage years of watching my idol George Michael on Top of the Pops. Wham, were my absolute favourites for sure and in his solo career George Michael was my all time Pop Star. His music resonated deeply with me. I adore music from all genres but as a young teenager Wham won my heart. The pop group wore "Choose Life" T-shirts, which sent a wonderful conscious and unconscious message out to the world. This took hold all of their fans. Everyone aspired to get hold of these T-shirts to follow the trend and be one with Wham.

For some it was a resonating feeling that they could choose life and how they lived it yet it did not mean they chose to do anything different. For others it was a fashion statement, there were even some fans who did not get the message it shared but had a knowing from within their Soul that it was important.

My team shared the understanding with me that it is ok not to always fully understand big messages like this at the time of your life that you do not even fully understand who you are. This was the case for me. At that young age I do not recall knowing exactly the reason behind George and Andrew's decision to wear this designer T-shirt, but I do remember how I felt. I felt a knowing of Hope within me. I felt a Desire for change. I felt a pull towards Freedom. I later learned the slogan came from Buddhism teachings as a way of raising awareness against war, death and destruction.

Choose Life is a powerful spiritual intention to guide you towards Choosing Love. Love will beat fear every time if it is chosen and felt.
The Spiritual Intention 'Choose' is so empowering when felt as it enables a shift within us for powerful change.

Just as I began to write this chapter my team told me to watch some Wham videos. The energy they shared with me filled my inner being with such vibrancy, fun and a freeing feeling. I felt the elation of the music vibrate within my physical body. My non-physical team were having a 'Danse' off that was for sure, but also the cells in my body felt the lightness of its energy and that vitality that it flowed through me. 'Danse' also being a Spiritual Term that I am able to enable and use to assist me to Flow through life and not worry too much about what comes next. Choose Life, Choose Love allows you to flow more freely in all you do. This is Self Love. This is enabling. This is wondrous. This is true flow. This is Magic.

The videos the team led me to were "Wake me up before you Go Go" an obvious first choice considering they already prompted the remembering as I held the vision of them all in their bright white T-shirts dancing on stage. Then I was lead to "Young Guns" and "Club Tropicana" All these tracks have high energy vibrations within them from the rhythm of the music and reflective lyrics of our life experiences. Also connecting me to a time when I did not feel the impact of lack of Self Love upon me. Feeling the knowing that when you Choose Love you open up opportunity for change of perception. A different view, a new perspective of how this experience can affect you.

George Michael went on to write so many powerful songs that inspire us to Choose Love in our life. Even though George struggled many times throughout his life to Choose Love for himself first. He knew it on a deep soulful level it was important, yet his life experiences made it hard for him to connect to this as much as he would have hoped to. He also had the additional pressure of living every decision he made in the spotlight of others. You each have your own spotlight to manage, be it loved ones, friends, colleagues, children, the pressure still affects you in the same way.
This disconnection from Self Love impacts so many souls on this planet. George was certainly not alone with the battle of unconditional Self Love.

⋛ SELF LOVE ⋚

Your Higher Self holds this love for you. They hold a pure positive highly vibrational unconditional love for you always. No matter what you have done, no matter what you have experienced, no matter what choices you have made or continue to make they love you unconditionally. This is a way in for you, to feel the knowing of this, for when it is hard for you to feel it for yourself you can ask and allow your magnificent higher self to share their love with you. Ask them to ignite the Self Love energy within you and start the flow of energy to help you when it can feel so distant from you.

My wonderful team and I have set the intention to amplify this connection for you. As soon as you set the intention with your Higher Self our energy will be with you. We are here with you always. It is our Desire to help each and every one of you to reconnect to Self Love in this process.

If only I knew then what I know now! Hindsight is not true energy. The truth is I did know then what I know now I was simply just too disconnected to feel it and remember it. This was how my journey was supposed to be I know this now, but I did get really frustrated about the hard times in my life. Oh why me I would ask. How comes everyone else is sailing through life and I am dealing with the crap. Why did I have to grow up, living my experiences that led me to not Choose Love for me on many occasions? This of course was my perception that everyone else had nailed life. When the truth is there are many people struggling with life too.

I remember hearing statements at school such as "Oh, that girl she loves herself" even though it was not directed at me I took on the emotions that loving myself was not the right thing to do. I was a young teenager holding the perception that Self Love was considered a fault not an asset.

I had no understanding of the difference between self-love and self-absorbed. I held a belief they were one in the same without a knowing of the impact that true Self Love has on our life; Physically, Mentally and Spiritually. Not knowing how to feel Self Love in the best possible way for my life here on Earth. Doing things for others that I did not want to do but did anyway with a fear of not being accepted, not being good enough, loved or allowed to be part of the group if I did not comply.

I found myself punishing my body as I held shame of how it looked because of the lack of Self Love and worth whilst thinking I had to be like everyone else. This included crazy diets, deprivation of foods, saying unkind things to myself and worse still allowing others to treat me poorly too. This is because I did not feel good enough as I held a fearful energy of comparison to others.

When you are not able to treat yourself with Self Love then how can you possibly put out the energy to receive the right kind of love back from others? This full realisation of conscious and unconscious habitual behaviours only coming to me in my 40's is of course better late than never and was also by perfect design. I now hold a knowing that it does not have to be this way either. Understanding this process opened up a new level of discovery of who I truly am and how wonderful and perfect I am right here and now. Yes, of course I can and will hold Desires to feel healthier and fitter within my physical body, but I will be setting these Desires for change from a place of Love rather than Fear.

There are so many people on this planet that feel that same way as I used to and missing out on the magical energy of Self Love. This realisation actually fills me with Hope for their change. The more intention myself and other like minded Souls broadcast out to the world this understanding the quicker our human race can align themselves to this way of living. Living consciously whole aligned with Love. I know if I can feel it and understand what it really means to me then so can you. I am excited for you to feel the truth in this.

I have a vision of the world connecting to self-love on a huge powerful conscious level. This energetic shift within physical human beings will shift the vibration of this planet to a whole new level. It is needed for expansion it is needed for regeneration it is needed for you to re-connect to your soul. It is needed for your purpose here on Earth. The Truth of You is LOVE. You hold within you the purest highest energetic vibration of LOVE.

Imagine our children growing up with this true understanding that Self Love is important and not selfish. Imagine a world where each and every person understood that Self Love stops Fear in its tracks from settling within our physical bodies. We need to stop the fear settling so it can no longer continue to cause physical and mental pain and suffering.

⟩ ACCEPTANCE ⟨

Self Love enables you to set boundaries to prevent others impacting you.
Self Love brings peace.
Self Love brings acceptance.
Self Love prevents habitual behaviours that cause addictions.
Self Love encourages you to keep going even when life throws those curve balls your way.
Self love will always bring your Soul back into balance, calm and true perspective.

Self Love enables Soul growth, which enacts your unique abilities for expansion. Yes, each and every human has unique abilities that are wondrous and exciting to understand.

Self Love enables your own self-healing. You can eradicate your physical and mental illnesses.

We all need Self Love. Every single human being on the planet needs Self Love. It is part of our Soul energy. We need it like we need food, water, air and connection.

This ripple of change will come from each and every one of you, as once you start to feel the shift within you there is no going back. You will also hold the Desire for those you love to love themself too. You cannot force this upon others, you an only hold the light on it for them. Once they see you blossom they will feel the truth of it too.

It is your life's work to love your self unconditionally. It is our life's work to encourage our children and our grandchildren to embrace and understand what Self Love means by setting the example.

I have a huge Desire to have this topic as part of the school curriculum, taught by teachers who embrace Self Love for them too.

A Desire for all employers to understand the importance of Self Love in the workplace because they too have a Desire to live by the Self Love code of practice. This would have such a huge impact on the mental well being in the workplace.

The truth is that Self Love is one of the easiest fears to understand, yet the hardest one to do, because the truth is we do not know how to put ourselves first. We are often consciously denying Self Love. We hold the beliefs that it will be frowned upon by others.

Are you always agreeing to do things you really do not
want to do?
Are you engaging with people who impact your vibration
and prevent you from choosing Self Love? Do you ever
say No and not feel guilty about it?
Are you doing a job that does not light up our soul?
Are you engaging in ways to narcotise your lack of love?
Addictions such as over working, excessive drinking,
eating, drugs, shopping etc. these are all distractions to
stop you feeling the fears you are holding on to, stopping
you from learning from them and letting them go.
Replacing these fears with love will truly dissolve them
out into the ether as explained in the previous chapter.
The common perception to consider is Self Love is NOT
Selfish. Now that is a powerful truth right there. State this
truth if you can with your Higher Self now if it feels good
to do so. The truth is it is not selfish to have Self Love.
If you have resistance bubbling within you then you have
work to do my darling. I know you know this already. You
are so ready for this change though. I can feel this
knowing from my team. We are here to support and guide
you through this process. Your Higher Self and team are
standing by ready to hold your energy through this.

Filling up your inner being with Self Love is the key to
truly letting go of the trip cycles and triggers that agitate
you on a conscious and unconscious level. It holds your
vibration into alignment so you can manage the tricky
experiences in good stead.

If you really want to feel change within you then you do
have to do the work. It can be tricky and feel icky for
some of the time but it will be so worth all your effort. On
the other side of this effort is the freedom to feel
incredible. Freedom to do all the things lack of Self Love

has prevented you from doing fully or even at all. Freedom to embrace the possibilities that will open up for you, as your energy shifts to a level like never before.

This wonderful energy of Freedom allows you to be you, the truest version of you, you in all your wonderful glory. Consider it as a system upgrade within your Soul.

Imagine the freedom that this brings for you. Allow yourself for a few minutes to connect with your Higher Self and ask them to generate the feeling of freedom of all the emotions of Self Love within your inner being. Your soul will light up, you will feel it activate and glow. You will be able to visualise yourself doing and being all you Desire.

Hold on to this energy for as long as you can. Feel it flow throughout your physical body. Your cells absolutely love this understanding. They are getting ready for this wave of Self Love to flow through it. They have wanted this. You have wanted this. Your Higher Self has wanted you to remember how awesome Self Love feels again.

It is not the responsibility of others to make you feel loved. This is your responsibility. Why would you choose to give this sole responsibility of the most precious thing you require to someone else? Love from others is of course wonderful and brilliant and magical, but so is your love for you. So is the love from your Higher Self and Non-Physical team. Do not give this responsibility away to others. Especially if those others do not have true connection to Self Love either. Allow the love from others to be a bonus, allow it to be a true energy exchange with so much joy. Not a love that only feels good when you are with them and crap when you are not.

How you feel is always your responsibility.
My biggest life lesson to date!

Self Love was my biggest understanding through my
awakening journey.
I had so many experiences where I had just let go of
compassion for me in each low vibration experience. The
understanding I allowed and beliefs I enabled as a
teenager and actually probably even before that in my
early childhood years, built up layers of Self Love
deprivation. This lack impacted how I showed up for
myself in school, work, relationships, as a parent, as a
friend, as a daughter, as a sister, as a wife. It impacted on
how I showed up for myself.

When I decided I had a desire for change, the lack of Self
Love would raise its head and hold me back from doing
all I desire to do. This lack of Self Love sabotaged my
dreams and manifested discomfort within my physical
body. The more I would feel the lack of Self Love the more
disconnected I got. It was a slow change but one of huge
compound affect. The undoing of this was a challenge for
me at times as it will be for you.

The Truth is Self Love will bring change on so many
levels. Following the releasing process will change all of
this for you.
All your fears stem from an experience that triggered lack
of Self Love either in that moment or thereafter upon
impact. It is important remember that this is not your
fault.

We get to 'Choose' on every occasion on every level how
we want to feel.

Your Creation in this very moment deserves the very best version of you. You deserve the very best version of you. The world needs the very best version of each and every single physical human and this version of you will only get better when you let go of the fears and live a life of love.
This best version is the truest version. The truest version of you was created in non-physical it is now time for you to remember how wonderful you already are.
We only get to live one physical incarnation on planet Earth.
Choose Love, Choose Life, Choose You.

⋛ THE TRUTH IS ⋚

Exercise ~ The Truth is.......

Once you have received from your Higher Self the understanding of the low vibration emotions for lack of Self Love you can set new truths about them in the Law of Truth.
Your guidance for these higher vibration feelings maybe for more Trust, Love, Hope, Truth, Strength, Courage, Confidence, Balance, Compassion to name a few.
Your wonderful Higher Self will guide you to the perfect truths for each experience.
Ask yourself, how will these new emotions enable you to feel?
What would you be able to do differently for yourself?
How will this impact the outcome of your Creation?

Stating high vibrational truths will replace the energetic gaps you have just made from letting go and setting the intention to dissolve. So go ahead now and fill these gaps with love labelled truths.

Here are a few to get you started.

The Truth is I am able to create all I desire the way I chose to.

The Truth is I am able to be flexible with my approach to creation if it feels good to do so.

The Truth is I trust myself to be successful in my creations.

The Truth is I am good enough.

The Truth is I am sharing so much hope for myself and for others with my Creation.

The Truth is my Creation is needed and therefore important.

The Truth is I am important.

The Truth is I am love and I allow my own love to flow through me.

The Truth is I have faith in myself to achieve success.

The Truth is I am able to make decision that make me feel good, allowing the best outcome for all.

The Truth is I can have compassion for my journey and allow myself to let go of the past.

The Truth is it is good for me to say out loud high vibrational comments to myself.

The Truth is my Higher Self loves me unconditionally.

The Truth is I am able to love myself wholly, Mind Body and Soul.

We love you x

Self Love Through and Through

I know, Self Love is a magical thing
Self Love will keep you from pain
Coz I've been there

I know, Self Love fills you up with Desire
Self Love cuts through doubt like a wire
Coz I've been there

I know, Self Love shows you the way
Self Love will not lead you astray,
Coz I've been there

I know, Self Love is pure and true
Self Love will never fool you,
Coz I've been there

I know Self Love opens the door to eternity
Self Love shows you all the possibilities
Coz I've been there

Allow Self Love in all that you do
Your bright light will always shine through
God is in there; we can all be there

~ Karen, Sarah & George ~
August 2020

≥ UNIVERSE DOWNLOAD ≤

⟩UNIVERSE DOWNLOAD⟨

ALLOW THE FLOW

Your Intention is powerful when you are aligning it to a specific targeted love labelled outcome.
In this instance your target is your Creation and it requires intention from your soul energy.
You have done so well to this point with identifying, understanding, letting go, dissolving fear based emotions and you have replaced all that energy with Love.

How are you feeling? Can you start to feel the shifts within you? Do you notice how you are reacting towards situations? You will start to feel a shift particularly around your Creation energy.

When you allow all you have come to understand to settle and Flow through your physical body you will get used to feeling better.
Allowing yourself to understand that you have released many Fear based experiences already and you have Let Go of the emotions connected to them.

There will be some habitual behaviour you need to be mindful of. Take notice when this happens and set the intention with your Higher Self to Live your truths.
This means your Higher Self will enact all your love labelled truths. It is good practice on a daily basis to apply

all truths as standard protocol for you as this helps you to align habitually to them.

It is time now for you to Flow with all you have come to learn and trust that the process is working for you. Yes there maybe more you need to release in relation to other aspects of your life, but what you have been brought to here and now is all by perfect design.

There are times when we can get so fixated on what else we need to do and not allow ourselves to align to what is. It is in this energy that you can allow the Flow to catch up with you and you with it.

⦚ CHILL ⦚

This allowing period is important, imagine it as the dust is settling on all you have uncovered and now you need to align your energy to the next steps.
Allow the Love energy you have generated within your inner being to really Flow through your whole physical body. See it and feel it going to where is needed to physically align too. It is like you and your Higher Self are calibrating your over all vibration levels. This is important and wondrous and healing is taking place for you. Awesome.

It is such a wonderful understanding and reassurance of the changes and confirmation you are doing so well. You can ask your Higher Self when this settling period has completed for you. It is important to just allow it, do not force anything as this will just ignite further resistance. It will serve you well to learn how to Flow. Flow is such a wonderful spiritual intention that really does not get enough credit.

Set the intention to Flow your energy with your Higher Self. You will be feeling this stronger now than ever before. It is such a wonderful relationship to nurture and grow. You can even set more truths at this stage if it feels good to do so especially in relation to allowing yourself to Flow more easily.

You can still take action on your Creation; you do not have to down tools just because you need to settle. Instead you need to go with what feels good. Therefore if it feels good to work on your Creation then do so. If it does not feel good then do something else. Allow flow to flow with you. You will be guided as to what is next.

Exercise ~ reflect upon how you are feeling when in Flow.

It is such a wonderful understanding and will help you realign to Flow when you are no longer experiencing it and Desire to.

Flow with Nature

As I look up and see
The sky's canvas looking at me
Sharing magical images
For all who are keen
Pinks and blues against the base of green
It amazes me always
This will never again be seen
Stay present in wonder and appreciate more
This Earth is incredible
Right from the core

~Karen & Sarah~
March 2020

≥ UNIVERSE DOWNLOAD ≤

≥ UNIVERSE DOWNLOAD ≤

IGNITE THE CREATIVITY

Logic tells us that ideas are formed in our conscious mind.
This is a logical thought and practical understanding.
Tick.
Just think about this understanding for a minute. Is it
really that straight forward?

Have you ever been in a meeting at work or in a situation
at home and you are asked to come up with an immediate
idea?
You find yourself sitting, thinking, thinking, and thinking.
All eyes are on you, you have a deadline to meet, come on,
have you got an idea yet? Your mind goes even more
fuzzy and blank and you just can't think. Oh the pressure
of an idea.

Nothing comes to you.
It's not like you can just pop up the menu page on the
television and a choice of ideas are there listed for you to
choose from.... or is it!

Ideas are a big energy influence in Creation. Creativity
desires interaction. It desires energy. It desires magic,
your magic.
It desires all of you, not just your conscious mind.
Creation requires your Mind, your Body and your Soul.
Yes all of you. You not only need to think it, you need to

feel its energy and you need to connect this idea with your soul. The idea comes from the truth of you and then combines with the truth of the possibility.

When that mind blank hits us, it is because creation has not engaged with all the elements it desires for the right outcome. Blimey, I hear you say, what other elements are there other than me having to think.
Your idea needs to engage with the energy of Creation to light up all the magic that it holds within it. Your idea already has the transform energy in it straight from the off. It also requires the energy of Magic. Magic can and will be generated by you throughout the creation process. Magic is a true energy held within the universe and we all have access to it if we allow it. Who would not want to engage with magic, especially when you feel how special it is?

⸺ MAGIC ⸺

To be able to influence the energy of ideas, you are required to exercise it like a muscle.
For it to get stronger you need to use it, to use it you need to allow it, to allow it you need to understand it, to understand it you need to accept it is even possible.
Some people have ideas flowing by the dozen and at a rapid rate. We have all sat next to that one person, in school or in the workplace. Some of us get a bit miffed with them because they are happily sitting there reeling

off the list of ideas they came up with in the first ten minutes of the brainstorming session. Others are sitting there in the meeting dis-engaged, as they had already set the belief that they will not receive any ideas as they remember all the previous occasion when they tried and got nothing, nada, not a single possible idea.

What they failed to remember though was how they felt on each occasion, that their energy at that time was also one of dis-belief, and the time before that and the time before that and so on and therefore their belief felt true. When they reaffirmed this truth the low vibration became stronger.

There were also occasions prior to that when they did actually receive an idea but it was discounted. Discounted not because it was not good enough, but because they didn't believe in their own idea in the first place. They didn't believe in themselves or their ability to achieve a good enough idea.

This low vibration energy was then held in their idea. Remember what I mentioned previously about your creation needing your vibration. They would then wonder why their ideas are never chosen once they have finally come up with an idea to offer. Why is it that Joe Blogg always had their idea chosen? It is not fair, they are always chosen over me. This then caused further low vibration and disconnection from the process. Joe Blogg's idea was chosen because they held the stronger energy of belief; therefore this energy attracted those who wanted an idea to believe in.

In this vibration of frustration and dis-satisfaction they now cannot wait for Joe Bloggs to rock up with their list and save the day and release them from this uncomfortable experience, they can then breathe a sigh of relief, and once again not engage themselves with the art of creating ideas. Phew they are off the hook again; until the next time that is!

The reason ideas have flowed to Joe Bloggs and probably not just one idea either, a pleather of ideas, is because they have allowed this aspect of themselves to be exercised, they have belief in themselves, they accept that they will always have the ability to receive an idea no matter what.
They would have started the exercise setting the intention that they will bring ideas to the table. They hold no resistance to the outcome. The have allowed the Creative energy to flow regardless. They are feeling rather happy with themselves too which raises the vibration and energy further of their ideas thus the energy continues to flow through the process. Note happy face of contentment from Joe Bloggs and it is totally deserved too.

This has now generated in us apathy towards this innocent person and towards ourselves for not being good enough. This energy will probably hang around for a while too. Not just for this meeting, for the next one and so on. We have created another fear-based memory around Creation for us to hold onto in our sub conscious and conscious mind. You can feel now how these everyday experiences can affect our vibration on so many levels.

The creative ideas list has been submitted and if one is only required then only one will be chosen. So all these other ideas do not become a reality at this point, and off they go back out into the ether for others to collate. So you see, even though all these ideas were generated does not mean they will all be used. However the energy of creating them will be used again and again by the person generating them in the first place.

Do you see now how this energetic interaction is so important to understand, as when you understand it you can allow it to flow with you.
These are always perfect opportunities for you to receive clarity on any experiences that you have encountered over the years that has generated low vibration in you that is preventing you from igniting your creativity.

Examples of these can and will possibly be in your every day life. When you want ideas on decorating for example. Do you struggle to visualize your ideas into reality?
If you were asked to come up with an idea of where to explore for a day out or designing a new layout for your garden, or even things considered to be as simple as ideas for dinner. Do you find this difficult also? Do you shy away from even exploring the opportunity to get creative? These all require the same energetic engagement so they are great ways to exercise this energy of Creation once you have identified some new truths around it.

When multiple ideas flow to you just note that not all ideas will be created. They will not fully engage in the full Creation process and therefore the possibilities of outcomes that are attached to these ideas are not illuminated so nothing else happens. I will share more regarding illumination energy soon.

For now, just know this, less is more. Therefore a basic truth to feel right now is that you do not have to always come up with a long list of ideas, to feel worthy of submitting any at all. You are here on this planet to create and co-create for the expansion of all for all many times over throughout your physical life.

⊰ ILLUMINATION ⊱

You are needed and your creative ideas are needed. You can exercise this ignition energy for creation with your higher self. Utilize it as much as you can on a daily basis in all aspects of your life. Feel the energy ramping up and all the energy of contentment reside within your inner being when you see yourself engaging with this process with more success than you have ever had on a conscious level.

Every time you see your list of ideas grow set new truths in the moment confirming that you are an awesome creator and you can generate amazing creative ideas whenever needed. Re-use this energy you have generated the next time you need to do this exercise again, this time remembering how you felt when you were in full flow with the energy of Creation.

It feels so good doesn't it?
Now that you have all these wonderful ideas of potential Creation, what to do with them?

Ignite Your Creativity

When I am next to the sea
I feel the energy rise up in me
I feel connection to possibilities
For you and for me

The expansion that awaits us
The opportunities to explore
The impact upon this planet
That's never been seen before

The more I feel into this
The truth of what I hold
I believe with my whole heart
That Love is growing bold

For all that really matters
Is to allow happiness to grow within
Then we can support others
To ignite their inspiration and begin

Unfolding the magic of what
The universe holds in store
Expansion for each and everyone
Of us to become even more

Its time to step forward now
Embrace all that has come before
Evolve the limitless growth
For now and forever more

~Karen & Sarah~
July 2020

AWAKEN YOUR CREATION

＝UNIVERSE DOWNLOAD ＝

≥ UNIVERSE DOWNLOAD ≤

CURIOSTY NEVER KILLED ANY CATS

Curiosity is probably one of the most under rated energies when it comes to creation. This incredible energy takes you to places that you may have never been before particularly in adulthood.

Did you ever find yourself exploring as a child, looking through boxes or drawers wondering what treasure you may find?
Did you ever go for a walk in the park and look at every thing there was to see regardless of how obvious it looked?

We would discover a piece of equipment and use it in every way possible even just a cardboard box. It could be a car, it could be a house, it could be a den, and it could be anything we chose it to be.
We would find a place to sit and look around even at blades of grass or insects in the ground, find woodland to explore and follow the hidden paths to see where we would end up, or maybe a sandpit to sit in and create castles.

As a child everything is wondrous and has so many possibilities.
Even asking the question "Why" holds huge amounts of curiosity energy. Yet as we grew older, we became more

120

familiar with our surroundings and took things for granted, stopped exploring, and were probably told off for asking the question "Why" too many times until we stopped.

Now I can't speak for cats as I don't have one so, but every time I take my dog 'Dottie' out for walks she will explore every inch of pavement and every blade of grass and every lamp post again and again, even though she has visited the forest or park a thousand times over, to her it is always like the first time. She always finds something new to explore, sniff, dig and genuinely look happy to be there.

The best part about the Curiosity energy is that by asking questions about what you discover opens up a thread of Intrigue, Desire and the deliberate conscious decision to explore further. Even the thought of doing this again already ignites this energy within you now. Can you feel it? It starts in your Hope vortex, and also connects in with your Truth vortex and a flutter of love flows through your inner being. This child like excitement is so wondrous and fun, but it needs to be exercised and let lose.

Curiosity is for creation in your daily life too. Curiosity took my family on an unexpected adventure a few years ago.

We were sitting at our table in Nando's having dinner where a discussion took place around my daughter finishing school much earlier the following year due to her exams. We were all discussing how it would be awesome to go to Ibiza for longer than our usual two weeks holiday. Then out of nowhere the curiosity energy flowed through my Hope vortex like a rumbling of excitement. At this point it is fair to say that I did not consciously know that it was curiosity energy, I was not even consciously aware of my Higher Self Sarah at that time, but she was activating this within me. I remember the feeling like it was yesterday and she is reminding me of this time for the purpose of this chapter. I do love it when she does this as it helps with my understanding too. Your Higher Self will do this for you to; they may already be doing it so just allow yourself to notice.

Back to the discussion over chicken, I then went into what I can only describe in a conscious dream state.

Paul and I found ourselves in a 'what if 'discussion. What if we went for a month, what if we could go for the full six weeks holiday and the extra weeks Danielle is off school. We were visualising our suntans, exploring the Island, feeling a sense of freedom for the whole summer, I remember even saying to Paul that I could smell the pine trees from the warmth of the sun.

WHAT IF

Conscious thought then stepped in and spoiled the vision, what would happen with our day job?
What about getting time off work?
What about how much money we would need?
Where would we live whilst there?
What if I saved all my holiday allowance and had unpaid leave could we afford it? What if? What if? What if?

I would dismiss the idea for a few days and then out of no-where this Curiosity energy built up within me and I could Feel See Hear Taste and almost Touch this experience of living in Ibiza for the summer. Surely it was possible.

This discussion went on for a few weeks. The Curiosity built up within me as I explored the possibility of the idea becoming probable. How could we make this happen? What would we need to do? And all the time I was visualising us exploring the wonderful Island of Ibiza, living a much-desired Spanish life. I did not let go of this possibility and neither did Sarah, she kept these thoughts and feeling ignited within me, as I now know it was all part of my soul contract alignment.

One afternoon whilst out shopping, I was led to a book, which had a chapter about sabbaticals in it. Right there in that chapter was my way to bring my creative idea of living abroad for a few weeks into the actuality of us living in Ibiza for six months. I had a concept of approach; Sarah had led me to this to show me the way.

The following year we had six wonderful months of living a Spanish life on the beautiful island of Ibiza, all because of a conversation over some tasty chicken. Of course there were many details and arrangements that needed to be made, as there will be with all creative ideas, but the truth is that by allowing myself to get curious and feel the energy flow within me, the more I did it the more I connected to it the more the probability of it being created was generated.

I felt the truth of my curiosity energy. My magnificent Higher Self 'Sarah' of course assisted me with this discovery and understanding. She helped me to hold my conscious thoughts back from saying "Don't be ridiculous, you cannot possibly just stop your life here in the UK and live in Ibiza for six months"!! Thank goodness she did, because we had the absolute best time. I was the crazy inventor who had the belief of my wonderful idea.

Yes there were others telling me it was not possible. What on earth was I thinking, but I held the belief and the truth that I felt when I allowed the wonderful energy of curiosity flow with my idea.

CURIOSITY

I did all this before I was consciously whole with Sarah. You can only imagine now what we are creating together alongside our wonderful non-physical team now that we are consciously whole. I am so excited for you too. This is such a simple but incredible realisation. You really are the dreamer of your dreams. You are the creator of your own destiny. You do not have to do this alone. You have your incredible Higher Self with you always. You have Sarah, our team and myself with you always energetically. There are communities of consciously whole physical humans who are waiting to support each other.
We are your tribe. We have got you. You just need to set the intention to allow.

Set the intention now to ask questions to your Higher Self about your creation idea such as "What if" and "If Then" and "Then What" these will get your conscious mind moving in ways that generates activity of possibility. You start to feel the energy brewing as you see the possibilities start to emerge from the answers to your questions and they flow through your mind like a film. The energy this creates ignites the desire to see more and feel more of what this possibility could bring to you or others. The possibility of change and the impact this creation would have on physical life and indeed the planet.

When the curiosity energy is in optimum flow it then triggers a pause/stop of your conscious thoughts being infiltrated by you like a dream state energy and this allows the possibilities to flow throughout your inner being connecting out to the universe igniting the energy of Hope for change within the Law of Truth, Law of Desire & Law of Synchronicity. Your Higher Self is doing this for you once you set the intention to be curious. There is also an element of influence from your unconscious thoughts that continues thereafter as your Higher Self continues this flow on your behalf keeping this connection flowing all the time you consciously connect to this possibility.

Remember when as a child there were no limits of possibilities. This is still true now when you can hold back your conscious thoughts from interrupting this flow these possibilities are on their way to probabilities.

When you consciously connect to this understanding you can actually feel this energy triggering this process within your mind. The curiosity energy allows your mind to consider other thoughts. It is so incredibly powerful, as you allow your mind to wonder across the energy of possibility just as a child would, without any care for reality in that moment. It would not matter if anyone said to you that your idea was ridiculous, you would continue to feel the truth of it in that moment and know that it was not ridiculous and absolutely possible. The truth is that you are able to generate incredible possibilities for Creation when you allow the full connection of the Curiosity energy to flow with you. In this process you are re-patterning your conscious thoughts to allow a spark of magic into your Hopes & Dreams.

This spark ignites curiosity without judgement from yourself in the first instance, but also without you feeling the judgement of others for your creation. You can feel the truth of it. This is why those people we would have considered as wacky inventors, keep going and going and going with their creative ideas until they crack it. They had felt the truth in their idea when they connected to the possibility energy through curiosity. Remember when I said I could Feel, See, Smell, Taste and Touch my life in Ibiza? I felt the Truth of this possibility.
The so-called wacky inventors are the same, they keep going and keep going until they ignite the activation of their invention. Thank goodness they did as look at all the incredible Creations that are out there in the world. They felt the Truth of it always and they aligned their energy to the probable outcome regardless of how long it takes.

This can also be true for you. Each and every one of us was born as creators of this universe. We are here to co-create with Non-physical and especially co-create with God. We agreed to do this as part of our soul contract. We agreed to this because we saw the possibilities for ourselves before coming into our physical incarnation.

We saw the possibilities of what this planet needs and Desires. All we need to do is remember how to do it.

We hold the energy of Creation with our Souls. This energy comes in the form of droplets of transform energy. Just as babies are created in the womb and they are grown with the transform energy from the tiny seeds of Hope. We too all have these seeds within us, when we truly allow and connect to the energetic capabilities of creation we ignited these seeds with Life energy and Magic.

We agreed to come to the Earth to create and expand the planet. The very first thing we created once we became physical was ourselves. For nine months or so we were in our mother's womb flowing with the energy of Creation. This was beautiful co-creation with our Higher Self, God and our mother of course.

Unfortunately most of us have had low vibration experiences that have disconnected us from this Knowing. This disconnection stopped us understanding the magic we hold within our Souls.
It is not your fault that this happened you must not hold blame for this, but now that you are aware, it can and must be re-ignited, as it is your responsibility to do so. Raising your vibration by letting go of fears will align your frequency to all your Desires.
If you have had previous experiences where by judgement from yourself or others has caused you to store low vibration then some simple truths with your Higher Self will enable you to start letting them go. You will continue this process throughout and as always your Higher Self will bring specific Truths to you in relation to your experiences. How awesome is this?

Even if you are already fully love labelled, your Higher
Self will bring you some perspective Truths to align to
and understand, especially if you are really pushing
yourself to the next level of Creation and expansion.
Something that is completely new for you will bring
conscious mind perspectives for you to navigate. You
know how to do this process you just need to be aware as
at times these perspectives can have unconscious
thoughts triggering them. So notice and ask your Higher
Self to bring them forward to you.

Here are some Truths to get you started.
Consciously connect with your Higher Self when doing
this and ask them to connect you to the Law of Truth.

The Truth is I am born a creator.
The Truth is my Creations are important
The Truth is I no longer need to hold judgement from
others or myself.
The Truth is it is ok to be curios
The Truth is I can ask why when I feel I need to
The Truth is Curiosity will ignite hope for discovery
The Truth is I can allow myself to explore just as I did as a
child.
The Truth is daydreaming is good for my Soul
The Truth is I can Feel, See, Hear, Taste and Touch my
Creation
The Truth is I believe in my Creation
The Truth is I believe my Creation is possible

Follow this exercise to ignite Curiosity with you

Close your eyes if you wish and relax.

Connect with your Higher Self and allow their wonderful energy flow through your Love vortex.

Share your loving energy back to them.

Visualise this loving exchange of energy between you both.

Ask your Higher Self to Flow their energy with yours and Ignite your Hope vortex.

Feel this ignition in your solar plexus.

This wonderful emotion of Hope is generating and building momentum.

Set the intention to target your Hope energy to your Creation.

Hope and Creation energy are magnetising together to build this Curiosity energy flow

Allow yourself now to explore your creative idea with the Curiosity flowing from your Hope vortex shining all over your idea.

Ask questions now to your Higher Self about this idea.

What if it did this, what if it did that? See if start to come to life.

What would happen then if it did this and what would happen then if it did that?

Feel its energy grow. Continue to ask these questions for as long as feels good for you. But do not rush it, as it is in this process you can see and feel what the possibilities are with this creative idea.

Ask your Higher Self to show these to you.

You may have more than one creative idea and that is ok too. Continue in this energy connection to get Curious about them all. This is such a fantastic energising exercise to do at any time as many times as you would like to.

This process goes beyond your usual visualisation techniques. It is even stronger than writing a daydream journal, although both these exercises are good to do too as extra if they feel good to you.

CO- CREATION

Your Higher Self is amplifying this Curiosity energy for you and with you. You are in the driving seat. You can expand this energy as far and wide as your imagination with take you.

What happens now that you are in Flow, Curiosity will stop your conscious thoughts getting in the way and allow you to really go beyond what this creative idea can evolve too. Your Higher Self knows what to do with this energy. It is an energy that you enjoyed with them all the time in non-physical. It is fun and you can have so much fun with it. When you are having fun you feel the Hope emit from your creative idea and connect to the freedom of the possibilities that flow from it.

Imagine now there are no boundaries at all.

There is no one saying that your Creation is not possible. You are now this excited inventor that you have witnessed maybe many times or have heard about and you are now connecting to their energy of Curiosity. Wow, feel this really flow freely within you. Your Higher Self is excited. Your non-physical team are excited. Are you now feeling this excitement too?

What if Thomas Edison did not persist with his idea of the light bulb?
What if Alexander Bell did not persist with his idea of the telephone?
What if Benjamin Franklin did not carry out scientific experiments to understand the nature of electricity?

The Truth is someone else would have instead. All of these possibilities were already waiting to be discovered and created by physical humans. It is usually those who believe in them and in their creations that are the ones who are able to take the credit for them.

Ask your Higher Self to connect you to the Law of Truth. Feel the truth in all you are seeing, feeling, knowing, believing, receiving, understanding and set these as truths now too. Feel the ignition of your Creation with this wonderful energy of Curiosity.
The Truth is anything and everything is possible when you believe.

Dis-claimer ~ to my knowledge there were no cats killed in the creation of this chapter or indeed at anytime they engaged with curiosity!

Wonder Full Life

The Wonder of wonder
When Hope is out of sight

The Wonder of the feelings
I connect to without fright

The Wonder of expansion
When it keeps me up at night

The Wonder of the healing
Wow igniting the power of sight

The Wonder of knowing
And the warm feels it gives inside

The Wonder of showing other
How to move their fears aside

The Wonder of connections made
Through attention to all within

The Wonder of allowing all the
Magic to set and begin

The Wonder of Nature
And all the lessons still untold

The Wonder of non-physical
And the stories they behold

The Wonder of colour
And what it means to you and me

The Wonder of food
And the creations of flavour that can be

The Wonder of resistance
And what letting go can do for me

The Wonder of connections
Made for all eternity

The Wonder of our animal guides
And the awesomeness they bring us

The Wonder of movement and that
It really can shift the surplus

The Wonder of energy
In all we see and do

The Wonder of 5ᵗʰ Dimension living
The Wonder of You

~ Karen & Sarah~
May 2020

UNIVERSE DOWNLOAD

≥ UNIVERSE DOWNLOAD ≤

HOPE IS AS BRIGHT AS THE SUN

Hope is one of the most incredible emotions to hold within your Soul, to feel it, to understand it and then to exercise it brings possibilities for change.

Hope has the power to change your perspective.
Your Hope vortex is in your solar plexus. This is where you can ignite and feel it. Your Higher Self will activate this for you when you connect to them and ask. You can ignite it yourself too but at times it can feel hard to really connect to it when your vibration is low.

When you find yourself in a position of sadness or despair it can be so hard to see your way forward. When you are holding a high level of low vibration emotions within your mind and body it disconnects you from your Soul. This makes it so hard to feel the Hope you hold within you. It can make it difficult to see your situation from a new perspective. When we are faced with difficult situations you may take it upon yourself to blame. This blame energy continues to drive a disconnection between you and your true self. Blame on you, blame on others or blaming life itself causes so much pain for all.

The Truth is it is not your fault. These experiences are part of your Soul journey, aspects of your Soul contract. No matter what this situation is, even if you instigated it, it is not your fault. We are reminding you of this with so much love. Your Higher Self is reminding you of this with utter unconditional love.

Perspective is the game changer for all situations. If you are able to generate enough Hope within you to even consider a new perspective, then this new perspective brings with it possibilities for change. This is what you Desire you Desire change. You Desire a way forward from where you are now. You Desire to feel Hope.

Hope is the ignition for change. From this new perspective brings respite from the despair. It allows your conscious mind to consider a new way of thinking. It allows your conscious mind to feel the possibility of a change of outcome. Your conscious mind is receiving a new energetic vibration from your Hope vortex. Within this vibration is a message. The message is from your Higher Self and from your Soul. The message is "Where there is Hope there is possibility. There are always a myriad of outcomes for all experiences" This message is often lost in translation because of your vibration at the time. The more you let go of low vibration the clearer this message will be received when you need it.

Even when you are fully love labelled, life will always share curve balls, tricky choices and closed doors. You are now so much better at receiving the messages from your Higher Self and your Soul and therefore you are able to navigate your perspective at a much quicker pace. This is the beauty of the releasing process as it stops you from feeling the fear that could be perceived which would normally then take over all rational thoughts. You are able to understand, you are able to allow it, and you are able to flow with Hope in a new-enlightened way.

From this place of respite you can feel the loving support and guidance of your Higher Self. They are always with you and are encouraging you to connect with them and ignite balance.
Balance is a state of being that will allow you to feel the possibilities of change with this new perspective.

Hope ignites the illumination for inspiration. This wonderful myriad of perspectives, changes and your possibilities will be illuminated with your Hope. You start to feel what these possibilities for change could bring for you; you start to see what they may look like and how you can align with them.
You are now able to engage the energy of Curiosity with these possibilities and see the illumination of the way forward. This is such an awesome feeling. Your Hope vortex goes bonkers with excitement. This is your Soul energy supported by your Higher Self. This excited energy starts to grow stronger and stronger as you begin to feel the probability of this new perspective and you feel the truth in it. More of this understanding and process is in the chapter of Curiosity.

Your Hope is feeling stronger which strengthens your conscious mind to consider the new perspective for a brand new outcome. You are able to 'let go' of the desperation you may have felt initially. The desperation no longer feels as true to you as it did before you felt a new way forward. This wonderful understanding of Hope allows you to move forward with love again. It allows you to feel connected again. It allows you to create a brand new story for your life's journey. It allows you to create your next chapter. Hope is showing you the way forward.

Hope holds the energy of Creation. When you are aligning to Hope in your Creation it allows your Creation to ignite life into it. Hope is the fuel for Curiosity. You are able to see your Creation expand with this magnificent energy. Your soul energy is filled with Magic. Your Magic is unique for you, yet it has a knowing of how your Soul is designed to use it. Your Hope vortex is the beacon for this Magic. It attracts your Creation to it. You feel the ignition start the life cycle within your Creation. It is time now to feel your Magic and allow yourself to step into your Creation with it. Just like you can step into the choice of possibility that you made. The possibility for a change of outcome to the situation you find yourself in.

⌇ INSPIRATION ⌇

Hope gives you the opportunity to choose your next step, to choose how you want to feel, to choose your outcome. Hope is your GPS within, your energetic navigation system to your next location.

Hope is the magnificent part of your inner being that pulls your Soul up and out from hiding who you truly are.

It is my Soul purpose to Ignite and amplify HOPE in You. It is my Soul purpose to Illuminate Your possibilities.

139

Hope is your fresh cup of positivity for your Life
Creations.
Hope influences the outcome of change.
Hope ignites a chemical reaction in the mind to feel there
is always another way each time you are met with the
opportunity for change.
Hope influences your behaviour. You influence Hope. Feel
the wonderful energy exchange between it all.

I too had to understand fully what Hope meant to me.
I have had many times in my life when I latched onto
Hope.
There were times when I just could not think of a way
forward in certain situations I found myself in over the
years.
I could not think it because Hope is not a thought, it is a
feeling, and it is an emotion therefore only when it is felt
is can then be really understood.
Hope is strong within me. It is an aspect of my Soul that is
so strong and the more I exercised it over the years the
more I was able to feel it.

I have always considered myself positive and optimistic
in my attitude to life. I used to believe it was my star sign
ha ha, I am Sagittarius, queen of positivity. It would be
something others that know me would say too. It is more
than just a star sign consideration, It is a Truth. It is a Soul
aspect for me. You all have many strong Soul aspects that
you will connect to and understand more through your
awakening. You may already know yours. Just know that
you have these for a reason. They become a strong part of
your capabilities to help yourself and others. They are to
be embraced, understood and exercised with Love.

My Hope vortex is so strong. I can literally feel it ignite within me. Like a flame igniting the gas cooker hob. This ignition has got stronger and stronger as I let go of low vibration fears through my awakening. This ability to ignite Hope now serves me more than ever before.

When I am ever faced with any choices whether they are deemed exciting or tricky I feel into the Truth of Hope, I set the intention to ignite it with my Higher Self and for her to show me the possibilities that lie ahead for me with this choice or situation. Hope really is your internal GPS system that will never let you down if you allow it to flow to you.

Ignite your Hope vortex and ignite the Magic it holds for you.

Hope is as Bright As The Sun

Hope is as Bright as the sun
Its vibrant yellow connects you to Fun
It is exactly where your frown
Turns itself upside down
Where rockets of Desire launch
In your belly full of fire
Hope is your navigation
Towards increasing your vibration
Your road map to the next station
Feel the emotion rise up within
Connecting to all your dreams to win
A life to host your miracles in
Hope is as Bright as the sun

~ Karen & Sarah ~
April 2020

≥ UNIVERSE DOWNLOAD ≤

UNIVERSE DOWNLOAD

ILLUMINATING POSSIBILITIES

Your Soul contract holds all your pre manifestations for your life here on Earth. All of these manifested outcomes you agreed to whilst in non-physical. How the manifestations unfold are down to you and the choices you make on a daily basis. Even what may be perceived as small choices such as when out driving which road you take when faced with left, right or straight ahead will bring to you three different potential outcomes. You really are the creator of your physical life and it is important for you to align to this.

You have free will to take your life in the direction you choose. If this direction is not in alignment with your Soul contract your Higher Self and your Soul will find ways to steer you back on course. They do this because you asked them to. Your Higher Self knows all you asked for and your soul holds the truth of you. Together they will bring to you a myriad of possibilities to choose from. It can be like finding yourself in a sweetshop filled with so many flavours. At times you can pick one flavour, other times you are indecisive and end up with a pick and mix.

There are times when we are being deliberate creators we ignite so many possibilities it can be difficult to understand and know which are for now and those that are for later on in your journey, and understanding some of these possibilities can be just a distraction altogether from your purpose. We will share more on how to manage your pick and mix in next chapter Spotlight.

The Truth is we do want to illuminate possibilities and as many that naturally flow when you are in the energy of Curiosity. The What if/if then process you have followed already will have ignited the potential that waits for you. You have allowed yourself to be guided by your Higher Self and the truth of you to places that fill your heart with so much love, joy and excitement. It is these possibilities that are already engaged with your Soul contract. You feel your Soul align with these possibilities. You feel the knowing of them. You feel the possibilities of probable outcome.

Many of these possibilities you have most likely felt before now. You may have dreamt about them in your childhood. You may have had fleeting moments in the past when you have wished that you were able to engage with them further. You may have seen others living aspects of these Creations and you felt your heartstrings pulled.
You may hold beliefs that you are not worthy of these high vibrational possibilities and that there is no way on Earth you would ever be able to do any of them. So therefore you do not even try. Until now that is!

You have received all of these possibilities no matter how far out of reach they feel to you right now because YOU are worthy. You are here to create all these possibilities and many more. You are important enough to align to these possibilities and make them probabilities.

I do get it. There have been fears getting in the way of your Creation. Do these fears feel a bit less impacting already than when you first started reading this book? I do Hope so. There may be some that you have not felt until now. There may be some connected to where it is you desire to be in your Creation that through this process have been brought forward to you by your Higher Self. This is good. You are feeling the fears that are preventing you from moving forward.

⹋ILLUMINATING ⹋
POSSIBILITIES

These fears are brought to you at the perfect time, as you now understand more about where you want to be. You understand more about how you can get there. You have seen and felt the future of your creation and how it lights you up. You understand what fills your Soul with Hope, Love and Desire. You also now know how to re-label these fears to love. You know how to set new truths to start releasing these fears. You do not need to let this stop you moving forward any longer. You are ready for this wonderful creation to manifest. This is your time to make it happen.

Many times throughout writing this book I have had to remind myself to live my truths. (Step 5 of the 'believe releasing process') I am fully love labelled yet I do have to remind myself that I too am worthy of all my Hopes and Dreams as I up level my Desires. These are new Desires and therefore bring new perspectives forward for me to contemplate. The Truth is, I too have received these possibilities to create and expand this universe because I asked to and God agreed.

There have been many possibilities on my life path that I know now were a distraction or even a mistranslation of what I thought I should be doing. Some of these were necessary at the time. I know now that Sarah, my Higher Self always had my back and always found a way to guide me to the right possibilities for my journey. Every time she did this it felt so good and my knowing grew with taking the actions.
Only when I consciously connected with Sarah was I able to receive clear guidance and understanding from her and my team as to where my soul contract is taking me.
I have seen and felt pre-manifestations that await me, which is so freaking exciting, and so can you. I have seen and felt the pre-manifestations that have already manifested and so will you. When this happens you can feel the truth of your illuminated possibilities. You can allow yourself to fully submerge into how they will feel, look, taste, touch, sound, experience. All your senses will come alive and flow through your Mind, Body and Soul in full alignment.

Find your space where this feels good to do. It may not always be possible to be there physically, but you can remember what you feel like when you are.
For me the beach calls my Soul, literally. I feel it pull me to it; it is where I Desire to be. It is not always possible but I am able to energetically be there. I allow myself to feel the connection. I visualise myself being at the beach, feeling the warmth of the sun on my face, the sand between my

toes. It is in this place I always feel free to do and be all I desire. This energy opens up the possibilities for me to engage more curiosity. Even though I am sitting at my desk right now and the cold December rain is saying hi outside, I can feel the flow of how I feel whilst at the beach.

Where is your place to feel this energy flow. It may be in the garden out in nature, it could be in the kitchen whilst cooking. It may even be just sitting still in a quiet room with a cuppa and allowing your self to just 'Be'.

Wherever this place is, go there; go there as much as you can when you are illuminating your possibilities. Go there and feel the energy flow through your Mind, Body and Soul. God is there with you. Your Higher Self is there with you. Your Non Physical Team is there with you. I am there with you. My team are there with you. We are all supporting these illuminations of possibilities, cheering you on, amplifying your connection and excited for you to remember why you are here on this planet, why your Creation is so important and why it is so needed.

Your Higher Self will bring some truths forward for you to understand in relation to this part of the process.

Here are a few to get you started

The Truth is I am able to illuminate possibilities for me.
The Truth is my Higher Self will guide these to me.
The Truth is I am excited to receive these illuminated possibilities.
The Truth is I am worthy of all these wonderful creative ideas.
The Truth is I am a creator and I am here to be creative.

Possibility Calls My Soul

The sea calls my soul
It magnetises my energy as I do to it
My vibration lifts even higher when I feel it calling me
The expansiveness it offers extends to eternity
The healing components are re-assuring me
I feel the rise and fall of the waves flow
As I feel my breath follow its rave
The colours are magnificent
The brightest blues and greens
The soft sand beneath it hosting
All who wish to dwell
Step forward into the waters
Of immense possibility
Allow the expansion of your soul
Towards how it is meant to be

~ Karen and Sarah ~
July 2020

⊰ UNIVERSE DOWNLOAD ⊱

AWAKEN YOUR CREATION

UNIVERSE DOWNLOAD

CREATION UNDER YOUR SPOTLIGHT

The ideas are flowing and you are excited by all of the possibilities you have received.
You have been bathing in the gorgeous energy of possibilities.
You are sitting there with your head back daydreaming about all the possibilities that they could bring for you. Every single one of them feels exciting and true and probable. You are already working out which order you are going to do them in and how quickly you can achieve this.

This is awesome, this is Creation, this is Magic, this is all your doing and you have exercised your Creative energy. It is simple but oh so effective. There are physical humans on this planet right now that do not even allow them selves to wonder what if, and you have done it in abundance. This Creative energy that flows through your soul is awesome and healing and expansive. Even if you had your creative idea before you started this book, I bet you this has now expended tenfold. I know this has brought an ignition of energy into it. I know that your Creation feels tangible and real. I know this creation has an energetic connection to probability more than ever before.

You have now entered the possibility party and you have limitless possibilities you are excited about. This feel so good doesn't it. This feeling ignites wonder and hope and fun and joy and so many other high vibration emotions.

Yay, I can crack on with all of them right?

Well yes, I suppose you could and you would be very busy indeed. However it does not mean they will all be successful. For the same reason as why not all ideas are used. They need to be fully engaged with the creation process, and if you split your energy over to many things at once the energy is not at its maximum strength. This will weaken the outcome.

"You can do anything, you just cannot do everything at the same time". This is a fabulous statement to remember. I did used to believe that multi tasking is and awesome skill. I used to think that the more I could do at once the more I would achieve. I thought it was considered admirable or hardworking when you can keep the balls juggling so to speak and have many projects on the go at any one time. Technically this is true, you would achieve more, but would you achieve the absolute best version of the outcome you Desire? Probably not, this is due to split energy and split focus and split priorities.

In order to gain the very best out come you are required to use your Spotlight energy to focus in on the perfectly aligned possibility to ignite first.
Which possibility is it that will be the one that is needed within the right timing? Which possibility is it that will be in the right place?
Which possibility is it that will be with the right people?

154

Synchronicity and manifestations are all part of the
Creation energy for success.
You have had all these amazing ideas, but it does not
mean they are all for you or all for now.

No matter how skilled you are at multi tasking and being
productive do not get sucked into the urgency of doing it
all at once.

The truth is multi tasking is not always what it is cracked
up to be energetically, if the tasks are not aligned with
each other's outcome then it will be counter productive.
Placing your energetic focus and activities around this
one clear possibility enables a more direct approach from
the Law of Synchronicity, Law of Attraction & Law of
Manifestation.
Spilt energy causes confusion to your manifestation
holdings and therefore the possibilities of success and
visibility will not be aligned accordingly and could take
much longer to manifest. You Desire a strong true energy
to connect with your current focus for success.

Spotlight is the beacon of light energy that unfolds from
your Hope vortex. You can feel it hone in on the very best
possibility for you to focus on right here right now. You
are the right person, in the right place, at the right time
with the right focus. This is the magic combination for
illumination and success. Feel the power of this
statement.

You are the Right Human, in the Right Place at the Right
Time with the Right Focus!

Your Higher Self will be guiding you throughout this

process. Set the intention to allow yourself to receive their guidance. Just because you may have received more than one possibility, does not mean that only one is the correct choice and the rest are red herrings. Far from it, you have received the multiple possibilities, because your Soul has called them to you. Each and every single one of them is with you for a reason. It is your job at this stage, together with your Higher Self to understand and allow the Spotlight energy beam on the right possibility for you in the here and now.

Take some time with this to feel into the probability of the outcomes, based upon where you are along your life's journey and Soul contract. This sounds complicated. It really isn't, but I do understand when you haven't done this before it can be a little daunting.

This is how we can help you. I say we, because not only do you have your Higher Self with you right now, you also have my Higher Self Sarah, my Non Physical team and our huge collective supporting you and holding your energy throughout this process. So lets do this.

Follow this exercise and you will engage with your Spotlight Energy to shine on your Creation.

Connect with your Higher Self and set the intention to weave your Soul energy with theirs. Really take the time to feel your energy combine and swell as they magnetize together.

Set the intention to allow the support of Team Hope View
to amplify this connection for you.
Feel into your solar plexus where your Hope Vortex is.
Ignite your Hope vortex and feel this energy expand and
flow with you and your Higher Self's soul energy.

Now ask your Higher Self to Illuminate your creative
ideas you generated from the Curiosity energy one by
one.

As each idea appears in front of you, feel, see or just know
a projection of Spotlight energy beam onto your idea. This
Spotlight energy will beam from your Hope vortex onto
your idea and engage in a priority energy aligned to
Synchronicity of importance.

You will feel a connection to each one of course as they
were all your creative ideas, however by doing this with
each one of the ideas your Higher Self will make the pull
towards you stronger for the order of priority. You may
even see this beam of light glow around your idea. This
confirmation of priority will come in the aligned ability of
how you receive the strongest from your Higher Self and
Non Physical team either cognitively, seeing, hearing or a
knowing.

Even if you had only one or two creative ideas Flow to
you when in the Curiosity energy still allow the Spotlight
Energy to beam onto it. As this energy is awesome and
not just to be used for a priority listing. Every creative
idea deserves the boost that the Spotlight Energy beam
will bring. This will allow the Law of Synchronicity to
align to its possibility and ignite Hope for this idea also.

The creative idea with the strongest pull to you from the

Spotlight energy is what will determine the priority of focus. Remember you may also pull towards you some off shoot ideas and these are all needed but focus on the main one first and then you can schedule in off shoot actions thereafter.

It is important to note that once you choose your most prominent possibility that the Spotlight energy shone brightly on and you felt the strongest pull from it, you then set your intention to stick with it and follow it through the rest of the process. Do not worry about all the other ideas you generated. You can keep these to one side for now and revisit thereafter.
For all off shoot possibilities from your current Spotlight Creation the action for these will flow accordingly so keep a note of them.

I should also remind you that energy changes, and therefore some or even all of the other creative ideas may not appeal to you at all when you revisit them and that is ok too.
Your Soul will have expanded by then, your stored vibration will have increased by then and the outcome from your first Spotlight Creation will have also changed the possibilities and probabilities of the other Creation ideas.

That is pretty awesome to know right? It feels really freeing to understand this.

Just because you felt excited about a creative idea does not mean you actually have to carry it out if it has not had the Spotlight energy beam on it as an initial priority. It will always be a possibility of course. It takes away the "I should still do it" feeling or "I should have done it before" regretful feeling. If these thoughts do come up for you then you can set some Truths around your perspective of this.

If you do not use these Creation ideas because you no longer align to them they will return out to the ether for other Souls to ignite should they still be required for Creation.
You can just let them go and take yourself through the idea generation process again with the magnificent Curiosity energy. I mean why would you not want to do that again as it feels freaking awesome.

Every time you do this Spotlight exercise your Soul expansion continues and your overall vibration will be at a completely different level, which is so exciting for the generation of your next creative ideas. You will certainly feel the difference with your connection, understanding, knowing and receiving from your Higher Self and Non-Physical guides.

Illuminate your current possibility with Ignition of the Spotlight beam of Hope and go for it. Give it your all and most of all Be Excited. We are.

Natures Spotlight

As the sun goes down
For you all to see
A day of reflection
For you and for me

The skies tell a story
That you'll not see again
But the memories you hold
To look back on remain

The colours of nature
Are never compromised
For nature knows all
For nature is wise

A new day is coming
For you to start a fresh
Let go of all you need to
Connect to new wonder instead

Summer Solstice is here
A beautiful night to comprehend
Just like Gods Love
Is with you and never ends.

~Karen and Sarah~
June 2020

UNIVERSE DOWNLOAD

≥ UNIVERSE DOWNLOAD ≤

HOCUS FOCUS

The wonderful Spotlight energy beam has shone brightly on your aligned creation and now it is time to give it your undivided attention.

You have created a wonderful idea and now you need to get started.
Have you started yet? What are you thinking? I will start tomorrow? I am not sure where to start? What if I get it wrong? What if I mess up the energy? What if I fail? What if? What if? What if?

What shall I go and do now to distract myself and put this off until another day when I feel like I know what to do?

I get it, it can feel a little daunting and overwhelm may kick in. This is perfectly normal so go easy on you. Just go off and do something else just yet.
Feel into these thoughts and emotions, when have you felt them before? Was there an experience your Higher Self is highlighting for you to understand more about? As they are a sure sign that you will have some releasing to do at this stage to be able to feel better about getting started?

By now you are becoming a master of the releasing process and setting Truths with your Higher Self that you can re-label these fears with Love and let go of what is holding you back.
So you can right now take some time to reflect and ask your Higher Self for some guidance as to what fears are triggering these emotions.
Tune in with your Higher Self using the connection practice already shared and allow the understanding to flow through.

There will be some obvious Truths that come up for you, there will also be some that will need further clarification and broader understanding too, so take your time with it. You cannot go wrong you cannot set too many Truths. Your focus is to feel the resonance of your Truths and allow them to settle within your Truth Vortex (tummy area). When you can feel them and they feel so good when you state them you are re-labelling these to Love.

There will be specific experiences that your Higher Self will share with you that will bring so much of this creative process together for you.
Now just because you have had these fears raise their head, does not mean you cannot take any action to start your Creation process. Some actions could be a new note pad for your ideas, thinking about a name for your creation. If you are starting a business you may like to flow with your Higher Self with ideas around logo. You may want to discuss your idea with a friend. You may have a desire to write a book and feel the nudge to start writing some outlive details about what it is about. Your Creation maybe a trip that is beyond your usual places for a much longer period of time, so start a Pinterest board, or internet search locations and print off photos. All of

these kinds of actions no matter how small will drive your focus and move the energy into your Creation.

It is important to get the energy moving, as when you do you will receive nudges from your Higher Self about what is next to re-label also in terms of Truths. It is important to know this is a process that will continue for some time, so have patience with you and your Higher Self. You are awakening and this takes time. Usually around 18-24 months for full awakening and you will most likely feel the Desire to keep going with the releasing process long after your Creation has taken place.

SETTLE
in your
TRUTHS

You are focusing on the re-labelling of emotions that come up for you in regards to your Creation there will most likely not be much more work to do thereafter that's for sure. However just know even doing this much is going to make so much difference to your happiness. When you allow yourself to go at the right pace which is always guided and supported by your Higher Self it will all take place in divine timing with true energy.

You are awakening, you are taking responsibility for your emotions, and you are doing what less than 5% of Physical humans are doing right now. How amazing it is to know you are aligning and allowing leading edge insight to live a happier and Love filled Life.

You are raising your vibration, you are raising the vibration of our wonderful planet, and all the while you are creating something unique and wonderful just like you. Feel the Truth in this. Feel the Truth of this wonderful process, as by doing so you will align to the Truth of You.

Here are a few Truths to get you started

The Truth is I am excited to start creating my possibility
The Truth is my Creation is going to be unique and needed.
The Truth is I allow myself to align to learning new skills to bring my Creation to life.
The Truth is I Desire for my Creation to become probability.
The Truth is I am ready to share my skills with a brand new audience.
The Truth is I can accept I will not have all of the knowledge I need to succeed, but I allow the understanding to flow to me in the right way.
The Truth is I will be able to make time to carry out the actions for my Creation.
The Truth is I appreciate that I will need to be kind and loving to myself in this process of Creation.
The Truth is it is ok to make mistakes, as it will guide me to a new approach.
The Truth is I can do anything I align my Mind, Body and Soul.
Staying focused on your Creation may become tricky at times, especially when we trigger a fear, so notice the signs. Remember our discussion about distractions. You can go back a read that chapter again if you find this happening for you and of course ask your Higher Self what are they bringing to your attention.

Many of us have this initial ability to stay focused upon our target. We can feel the excitement and feel the energy rise up within us as we get started on bringing our creation to life. Energise these emotions allow then to run through you and around you.

You will find your own unique way of taking action in terms of what methods work for you best. Just know you are on the right track when you have your focus aligned to your Creation.

creation with
— WONDER —

If you find you have a sticking point with what actions to take next take yourself back to the Curiosity energy but this time with your specific Creation as the focus. This wonderful energy will show you the incredible possibilities that your Creation will engage with. Allow all of you to flow with this energy and see yourself taking actions to ignite what comes next.

It is such a fun way to align you to the Truth of your Creation. When you drive focus you will energise your Creation. Your attention and intentions will expand its energy.

Align your actions only to this creation do not be tempted to think that if you had chosen one of your other possibilities it may be easier to do or you would know where and how to start taking action.

The Truth is you have chosen this Creation because your Soul pulled it to you. Your Higher Self is lining it up within the Laws of Synchronicity to bring the heightened energy to you so you felt its pull.
Energetically and physically step into this Creation with focus, excitement, anticipation and wonder.

It is going to be awesome.

Focus with the Universe

When I stand at the ocean
And look out far and wide
I feel connected to so much wonder
I can feel it brewing inside
The ocean is endless
Like the possibilities we hold
So lets get focused onto
What the Universe can unfold

~Karen & Sarah~
March 2020

≥ UNIVERSE DOWNLOAD ≤

≡ UNIVERSE DOWNLOAD ≡

THE TRUTH OF YOUR CREATION

The Truth is your Creation has already been agreed and planned by you in Non-Physical. The Truth is you wanted this. The Truth is you asked for this.
The Truth is you have a Soul contract that you agreed to achieve whilst you are having your Physical Life here on Earth.

I have the pleasure and privilege to share details of Soul contracts with my clients and the wonder that comes through for them is always so awesome. They get to understand certain milestones they have already encountered and those yet to come.

When we choose the light path of our journey and particularly when we live it consciously whole we start to ignite the wondrous aspects of what lies ahead for us. We become deliberate creators with the universe.

The higher your vibration becomes the clearer the understanding you can receive from your Higher Self as to what your Soul contract entails. This really helps you connect to the Truth of your journey and the Truth of your Creation.

The finer details of your Soul contract are always down to you to create once you are here in physical with your own Free Will and the choices that you make on your life's journey. For example you may have asked for notoriety in this lifetime, but how that comes about could be from any experience. You may have asked for the most wonderful loving family, yet this could be in connection to a club or project you undertake or through adoption or fostering for example. You may have asked to make an impacting change on the planet, yet this could turn out to be by creating and invention that helps millions save plastic waste. Ultimately there is an overall experience that you asked for in fact many experiences and they are all waiting in the wings for you to align to the right energy, time, place and people.

There are many times we are just far to busy being busy that we miss the signs from our Higher Self and Non-Physical team that are guiding us to a place of ignition. Igniting the creation that awaits you. It is my Hope that this book becomes one of the biggest signs that Physical Humans have been waiting for. It is my Hope that this book is a sign and a support guide to ignite your possibilities. This book is a way of allowing you permission to go for your Hopes and Dreams. That this book shows you that anything and everything is possible and that all you need to do is align yourself to the right energy frequency to attract it to your reality.

Thoughts really do become things!

I never ever had any thoughts about writing a book up to about a year ago. My Higher Self started bringing me poems. It all started in early March 2020, I was sitting at my desk staring out the window and I felt the urge to pick

up my pen and start writing. The poem just flowed. I did not stop until it had completely finished. I did not have to tweak it or re-write any of it, it was done.
It felt awesome, I felt awesome, I shared it in a social media group I was in and that was that. I had never written a poem of substance. To be honest I had not felt any Desire to do so. But when this first download came and I could feel the energy it held within my Soul I felt a Desire to receive more. More came from Sarah my wonderful Higher Self and we had found an awesome way of communicating. At times other Non-Physical entities would join in too.

I was in awe of the process. I shared them on my social media platform because the messages felt important.
It was not until I had started the process of writing this book that I truly understood their purpose. Many of our poems are in this book. I started writing this book in November 2020. I had received over 35 poems by that time.

This book came about from allowing myself to accept that I am here for more and with the encouragement from my Higher Self and from my mentors and peers and lots of Truths of course. I am here in this physical incarnation to achieve my Soul contract and more. I am here to turn my possibilities to probabilities. When I set out writing the book I did not have the full picture about what it would be about and yet I started writing. I felt the Truth in the outcome and with this the outcome flowed to me.

Your creation is all part of this experience at this time of your Soul contract and you have reached a milestone of bringing it into manifestation.

Now try not to agitate or feel any pressure of this understanding as you can cause resistance and slow down the process of manifestation.

Instead, if you are feeling the pressure of this understanding then you know what to do. Feel into these emotions with your Higher Self so you can understand what is triggering them and then set some new Truths.

There are a few Truths at the start of this chapter that you can state, and more will come for you too once you connect in with your Higher Self.

The resistance will be more than likely due to a few considerations.

~It may be that you are still yet to fully trust in the process.
~Maybe you are not trusting yourself to complete this wonderful Creation.
~It may be due to judgement from yourself or others that you will not do a very good job or see it through to the end.
~It could be the fear of not fully understanding the aspects of the Creation and what its purpose is for.
~ You may think you need to know the full details right a way.

~It may be a resistance to becoming more visible.
~You may be holding a lack of worth in the outcome of
this creation.
~It could be that you feel you do not deserve the success
that it may bring your way.

These are just a few considerations to ask your Higher
Self to guide you on if you are yet to really connect with
the Truth of your Creation.

Thoughts do become things! Fact! My book was a thought
and now it is a thing.
Action makes this happen. Making the choice and taking
the action allows the outcome to flow to you.

Energy attracts energy, we are all energy and all things
are energy. Throughout this process you are aligning your
energy to the outcome you desire for your creation. Your
creation is energy. Your emotions are energy. All Creation
is energy. These words are energy and my enthusiasm
and excitement for your Creation is energy. It is safe to
say everything is generating energy. Your thoughts ignite
it, your emotions amplify it and your actions will build its
momentum.

The basic understanding of Law of Attraction is that you
will attract back what you give out. To attract what it is
you Desire you need to accept and align your energy to
what it is you Desire. You need to set this Desire from the
highest vibration frequency within you and really allow
that energy to flow through you and with you in your
expectation of manifestation.

You more than likely know all this already, but do you feel it?

This aligned energy of Hope, Desire, Love and Wonder that you hold within the Truth of your Creation is what you are here now to align to. See it, feel it, be it.

Remember thoughts will become things if you feel them to be true. The timing of its arrival can and will depend upon the dependencies you hold around them.
So if you are really not feeling the Truth of your Creation then how can you attract the energy to bring it into manifestation?

Remember the mad inventor analogy?
No matter what anyone said to them they knew it to be true. They held a strong knowing and all they needed to do was to stay aligned to this energy and the Truth would unfold.
Once you have cleared the resistance at the stage with your Higher Self, ask them to ignite within you the Truth of your creation. Allow this wonderful energy to flow with you and through you. Go deep within your Soul and see, feel, hear, taste, touch and be all in your Creation.
Experience it in action. Experience the magic it will bring Experience the importance of it. Allow the importance for you and for others.
This is The Truth of your Creation.
The Truth is there is so much Love to be found in your Creation

Love is waiting to be found

Find the Love that resides in you
Find the love that others see is true
Find the Love that holds you tight
Find the Love that gives you sight

Find the Love that ignites Hope within
Find the Love where life begins
Find the Love for all to share
Find the Love that stops and stares

Find the Love in all you say and do
Find the Love that pushes you through
Find the Love that brings Joy to all
Find the Love that rocks your Soul

There is Love for all,
In all when you allow it
It's not really hiding from you
You just forgot where to look for it

~Karen & Sarah~
September 2020

UNIVERSE DOWNLOAD

≥ UNIVERSE DOWNLOAD ≤

MAGNETISE YOUR DESIRE

Now it is time to really juice up your Desires for your Creation and allow yourself to really flow with its awesome energy.

When reading through this chapter, consciously connect with your Higher Self. Once you are in a strong connection, ask your Higher Self to connect you to the Law of Desire. This is a wonderful Spiritual Law that you connect to for manifestation.

In this law you set Desires with a capital D. Desires with a capital D are the desires you truly long for, the ones that fill your heart with so much love and joy. Strong powerful Desires are the ones that will bring tears to your eyes with the having of it. Desires are exciting, they bring change, and they are wondrous. Desires with a capital D are not just "that would be nice to have or do Desires"

The Law of Desire holds the most delicious energy. It sure is one of my favourites. It works along side other Laws of the Universe such as Law of Attraction and Law of Synchronicity and will magnetise your manifestations to you at pace.

Imagine you are wearing a virtual headset and as you switch it on you are IN your Creation. Ask your Higher Self to assist you. Ask them to 'Hold' any low vibration infiltrating conscious thoughts at bay so that you can fully step into your Creation energy flow.

Visualise yourself in the midst of your Creation in full action, in full operation, see yourself using it, see others using it too if appropriate. See the end result of your creation in all its glory. Feel the possibility of your Creation becoming probability. See its potential to grow and become stronger. Feel its energy of transformation flowing with all who wish to experience it.

Take a look around, are you in a particular location with this creation, what does it look like, what can you Smell, See, Taste or Touch? Is it in a different country, on the beach, maybe in a new home, or a new company building? Is it a creation for children or adults? Is it a new revolutionary App or gadget that will change the world? Can you see it on the TV or hear about it on the radio? Really get detailed about it and see it come to life.
What are you wearing? What does your day look like in terms of the actions you are doing? Are you meeting new clients, or are you trying on the dress of your dreams?
How do you feel seeing this creation completed?
It is your Creation go for it, all bells and whistles, no restrictions, allow yourself to submerge in the intensity of your Desire.

What is it about your creation you really Desire to experience?

What can you see yourself doing differently as a result of your Creation?

How can you help others with your Creation and what difference is it going to make for them?

This is not a process to be whisked through at pace. This is an experience in itself. Connecting to the Law of Desire, setting the intention for your Higher Self to amplify this experience for you and go ALL IN and of course now that you have revved up this energy, invite the energy of Curiosity in to really get your party started. Curiosity and Desire oh my what a magical combination of energy for change.

Ask out loud some What if questions and feel the curiosity energy light these questions up. Allow time between each statement for the energy to flow within you. Do not worry to much if this is still feeling new and you are not really feeling the energy just yet, just hold a knowing it is happening.

What if my 'Creation' engaged with 1000's and 1000's of people?
What if my 'Creation' changed these peoples lives for the better?
What if my 'Creation' changed my life to be able to live it with Freedom?
What if my 'Creation' helped me live each day in the future doing all the things I love to do without any restrictions?
What if my 'Creation' evolved to helping people globally?
What if my 'Creation' improved my health and wellbeing?
What if my 'Creation' improved the health and well being of others?
What if my 'Creation' impacted upon the improvement of our planet?

What if my 'Creation' allowed me to be the happiest version of me in each day?
What if my 'Creation' enhanced the relationship between my loved ones and me?
What if my 'Creation' helped my family live a life of Freedom and Hope for the future?

Ask as many What if questions as you Desire, ask whatever What if statements come to you as they will be specific towards your Creation. The important thing to do is to FEEL the Curiosity energy flow within every single statement and the wave of energy that flows back to your from your Higher Self and your Non-Physical team. This energy is confirmation that these possibilities are able to become probabilities. You may feel a knowing, you may hear or see this confirmation. It will be unique to you based upon your own capabilities. Intention is what engages it so feel the Truth of each one as you say them. I must also say that by saying these statement out loud and all Truths for that matter, you will feel the vibration of your words so much stronger than saying them in your mind.

I can feel this energy now ramping up within my inner being as I ask my Higher Self Sarah, to ignite this within me, as I Desire to feel this energy right now to help me see and feel your Higher Self and your energy in this understanding. It feels flipping awesome. It feels empowering. It feels magical. It feels relatable. It feels flipping awesome, oh yeah I said that already, but I am just going to sit here in it for a little while with my Non-Physical team and Harness it and allow it to flow through me and around me like I am in my Creation bubble and feel the possibility of it all.

All my senses are on full power and I can feel the energy of this book now engaging with probability energy. I can see and feel the energy of Hope really ramp up within me now; I can feel it ignite in my solar plexus. I can feel the energy of my Non-Physical team as I ask them if I am translating this understanding fully so I can share it with you.

I have a huge Desire for as many people as physically possible to read my book and feel the huge energy of Hope that glides throughout. The Hope for them, the Hope for others and the Hope for our wonderful planet. It is in this Desire energy weaved with the Curiosity energy that I can feel the probability of change. I can see the cogwheels turning as the Right People, in the Right Place, at the Right Time are igniting their Creations. I can feel the Law of Desire, Law of Attraction, Law of Manifestation and Law of Synchronicity all in cahoots to make this happen. It feels frigging awesome.

Now you are feeling all the high vibrational feels of the possibilities you Desire about your Creation, go all in and ASK your Higher Self to ignite this Desire with a capital D and feel the Love of it, Feel the Hope for it, Feel the Truth of it and Feel it Strengthen within your Ask. Oh My, really feel this Desire energy ramp up throughout your Mind Body and Soul.

This is no ordinary Desire this is YOUR Desire with a whopping capital D and doesn't it feel so good. Do not let go of this feeling just yet, now set the intention with your Higher Self to Magnetise it towards you. Adjust your

Virtual headset and focus because your Creation is coming closer, and close and closer to you.

Can you feel your probability energy igniting?

Feel its energy attract to yours. Feel it magnetise towards your high vibration frequency and now call in the Law of Attraction.
The Law of Attraction will now co-ordinate its frequency with the Law of Desire, Law of Manifestation, Law of Synchronicity and start chartering this possibility towards probability, however you need to ensure you hold the energy of Desire until your Higher Self confirms your Desire is in place with all the other elements.

If at any time your connection to your Desire starts to dip, as of course it will at times when life happens and when you are navigating your way through actions, connect back into this process with your wonderful Higher Self and flow with this Desire energy you created again, and again and again as many times as you need to until your Creation manifests into reality.

Remember what I said earlier on in the book, you cannot just sit back and leave it to the Universe to manifest for you, you are the Universe and you need to play your part. Yes the Laws of the Universe will support this manifestation of your Creation and your incredible Higher Self will guide and support you too, however you must take action. You must follow the inspired actions and opportunities that will for sure come to your door.

ASK your Higher Self for help and allow the support and guidance to flow to you.

Keep your virtual headset close by, as this is your access to seeing and feeling your Desires that your Creation is going to bring to you and keeping them at the right frequency taking them from possibility to probability.

There is so much more detail about the Law of Desire in 'believe" by 5th Dimension Earth and I urge you to find out more as this insight is incredible and life changing for all.

I am just going to sit here for a bit and bathe in this energy for a little while longer as it feels so so good.
God is at work here. God Desires for you to create and co create with others.
God is the King of all Creation just look at this wonderful Planet we live upon. That is Gods handy work. Nature is the next in line in my opinion, in terms of Creation.
Nature creates and co creates in every second without any fear.
Its consciousness just knows what to do.
If there is something in its way, it will find a way around it.
No moaning, no complaining, just acceptance that this is what needs to happen. Acceptance that this is what it is here for.
Just like you and I and all those other billions of physical humans we are designed to ignite the Desire for change and Create Magic in our own unique perfect way.
All we need to do is let go of the Fear that is preventing us from doing so, and create magic with Love.

A Dose of Desire

The Energy is always higher
When we ignite a dose of Desire
We are here to create with Love
Enabled by our consciousness from above

The creations we make are always guided
We already have the details provided
It is now down to us to Remember
From way back when our Soul was in the ether

The universe holds all the answers
It says we'll give you the signs when you ask us
Go deep down within and let the Fun and Magic begin
So our wonderful planet can vibrate higher even faster

~Karen and Sarah~
January 2021

≥ UNIVERSE DOWNLOAD ≥

≳UNIVERSE DOWNLOAD ≲

TIPPING INTO PROBABILITY

Lets get the party started, and tip your possibility to
probability.
This is all about action.
We touched on it briefly before and of course you may
have started taking action already, and this is all by
perfect design.

This chapter is really about getting you to feel into your
actions. You have seen the incredible possibilities that
your Creation can bring for you, and you have felt its true
energy and you have a knowing of it becoming a
probability but it takes action.

Choice + Action = Allowing

Allowing the guidance to flow to you.
Allowing the opportunities that come your way to be
considered.
Allowing the nudges from your Higher Self as they
confirm to you the next steps.
Allowing the support from people or places that you do
not normally interact with.

Remember why you are here now in this moment with
your Creation and Choose to take Action.

There will be days when you do nothing and there will be days when you are inspired to do lots. Just know that each day will bring to you the right actions at the right time, but you must allow them.

There will be times when your actions make no sense at all at the time, still allow them as their reason will unfold. You need to Trust the process. There may be actions you took a while ago that now actually fall into place. Maybe you signed up for a training programme and completed it and it is only now that you will get to utilise the knowledge from it.
Maybe like me you were receiving information ages ago that you will understand how it fits in now.

Do not underestimate the amount of unconscious preparation you have already had going on towards your Creation, as everything you have done up to now on your Souls journey will all form part of your overall Soul contract.

You have not just been 'Awakening your Creation' you have been 'Awakening You'. Through your wondrous connection now with your Higher Self you have understood so many aspects of your life. They have helped you understand why you feel the way you do. Your Higher Self has shown you how these feelings and emotions have been affecting you. Your Higher Self has supported you and will continue to do so always and they have ignited your intentions for change. By allowing yourself to re-label your Fears to Love by following the believe releasing process you have raised your vibration and let go of what no longer serves you.

You are well on your way to Emotional Freedom. Feel the Truth in this. Feel the possibilities that this can bring for you.
Feel the Freedom that awaits you.

You have started a wondrous relationship with your Higher Self and you quite possibly have received guidance from your Non Physical team too. For some of you this will be the start of this amazing awakening journey and you still have so much more to understand and let go of, but I know you are already starting to feel the change within you. Keep utilising the 'believe' releasing process and setting Truths as you take the actions for your Creation towards success.

For those of you who have either already started the awakening journey or are fully awakened I believe you will now be receiving further insight on your abilities and how you can utilise them within your Creation. This feels exciting for sure. Even when we become fully love labelled we are still having a physical experience and therefore Life will still bring us new experiences to have a perspective of. A Fear based perspective or a Love perspective it is of course down to us to make the choice of how we manage them. Choosing Love always will allow these experiences to flow through our journey of life with more ease and grace. Calling in the Law of Balance and then calling your Truths will enable you to choose from perfect vibrational space.

Of course you not do have to just have the intentions for Creation to continue your Awakening journey, but it sure is a fun way of doing it, as it means you can move forward with change along side letting go of low stored vibration.

Your next Creation may be something completely different or it may naturally flow from the last, either way you will continue to bring new energy into the ether and energise and raise the vibration for all.

In order for you to fully reach your energetic tipping point for Creation will mean you consciously flowing with the actions and have the intention that each action ignites further change towards the outcome. Each step you take visualise this igniting another aspect of your creation, maybe have something visual for you to track it and feel this expansion within your Creation.

When I first set out to write this book I received a list of spiritual intentions from my Higher Self and my Non-physical team. The team asked me this question.
What if this book was an Energetic Sequence?
I realised that the list of spiritual intentions would form a sequence of events to which I would then write about in a form of process for you to follow. Upon me writing each chapter the content was guided by the team. I did not write the chapters in order of sequence though to start with. As I received the guidance I wrote down what flowed naturally. It was only when I had the broader understanding as to what this book would be about did I then stepped into the sequence for completing each chapter in order.
So you see, your Creation actions will flow to you in the appropriate way for you, but it does not always seem obvious at first. Do not discount anything you receive as guidance, as it will all have its place. Trust in yourself, Trust your Higher Self and Trust your Non-Physical team. If this is now flagging up some further Truths for you to set around receiving guidance in this new way then go ahead and set them. It takes time to adjust to working this

way, it takes time to adjust to receiving from your team so go easy on yourself and allow it to come at the pace it does. When you feel impatient or try and force the receiving of information it can and will most probably just slow things down, because you will be engaging with low vibration so it will block the tuning.

If you find yourself at a sticking point then just allow yourself some slack and go and do something else and come back to it. Remember energy changes, for you and for your team too, so either stop working on your Creation for a little while or work on a different aspect of it. You will find that as soon as you change your energy around it with what you are switching your focus on the guidance will then flow through. If you are anything like me I receive insight when I am balanced, when I am in the shower or when I am having fun. Go with what feels good for you.

The list of Spiritual intentions I had listed went on to create the contents list for my book. I was able to then use this list to visually see my progress. As I made my way through the list I could feel the momentum building and the possibility of me writing a book tipping over into the probability of it being created, published, printed and bought by you gorgeous ones.

Find your own way of keeping track of all you are doing and seeing the momentum build. Stay persistent and consistent. Allow yourself some time each day to do one aspect of the Creation. It does not matter if it is 5 minutes, 1 hour or all day, you each will need to work the time you have available into your schedule, but do something daily. The connection you have with it each day is important. It is the energy of your connection and the energy of your actions that builds the momentum of your Creation.

The Spiritual Intentions that I received when I started writing this book formed an energetic sequence that you are enabling upon completion of each chapter. My Higher Self and Non-Physical team are enacting this for you with your Higher Self and your Non-Physical team and in a collaboration of the sheer power of energetics your Creations are igniting in your Manifestation holding.

Understanding the sheer Power of Energetics and how when you use them can change and influence you in so many wondrous ways is another book entirely, however you can find out more if you are already intrigued at 5thdimensionearth.com

The energetic sequence you are enabling is enabling you to be at the right vibration for you to attract your Desires for your Creation to manifest.

❖ The trip cycles you have understood have been released to bring your vibration into balance.

❖ The disruptors causing low vibration you have released is allowing your vibration to align to the Desire of your Creation.

❖ The letting go of fears has enabled you to do things that you had been shying away from because you were being held by the low vibration emotions and just could not bring yourself to do it.

196

❖ The dissolving of old beliefs are no longer pulling you back to fear.

❖ You have an understanding of how Balance aligns your Mind Body and Soul to allow you to feel more.

❖ Choosing Love for you in each moment is attracting the same loving energy you Desire in your Creation.

❖ Allowing yourself to build a wondrous relationship with your Higher Self is opening up your connection with the Universe.

❖ Igniting your ideas and illuminating possibilities is opening up your conscious and sub conscious mind to opportunities that await you.

❖ Calling in the wondrous Curiosity energy to allow you to explore the infinite possibilities that are waiting to flow your way.

❖ Activating Hope within you, is allowing your conscious thought to ignite the feeling of possibilities to become probabilities. your possibilities indicating to the Laws of the Universe that you are feeling their pull towards you.

❖ Opening up those flood gates and allowing yourself to engage with these illuminated possibilities and letting yourself to flow freely with them.

❖ Beaming your incredible Spotlight energy onto the right Creation for you at this stage of your Soul contract.

❖ Staying focused on your Creation is building momentum within the Laws of the Universe to pull your Creation to you.

❖ You ignited and felt the Truth of your Creation, engaging the Laws of the Universe for confirmation.

❖ Connecting to the Law of Desire weaved with the energy of Curiosity to allow you to really feel the Desires and the satisfaction of having them.

❖ The actions you take are tipping your possibilities to probabilities.

You are doing something in a way that less than 5% of our current population are doing and that is Consciously Creating with the Universe and expanding yourself and our incredible Planet and Beyond.

We are so proud of you and remember we are with you energetically every step of the way.

≥ UNIVERSE DOWNLOAD ≤

≥ UNIVERSE DOWNLOAD ≤

JOYFUL TRANSFORMTIONS

Feel the Joy that flows with you throughout your wondrous transformation.
Pocket these high vibrations into a Creation bucket with your Higher Self.

When you are setting any Truths your Higher Self can categorise these for you, all you need to do is ask. So throughout your Creation Journey when you are feeling the Joy in your understanding, in your actions, in your results, in the unfolding of your manifestations, in the Creation of your Possibility feel this loving, hopeful, joyful energy ignite within you and put it into your Creation Truth Bucket.

You can then call these high vibrations to you at any time you Desire. You can call all your Truths at the start of each day or before you engage with your Creation so that you can feel the power of all the energetic change you have encountered already.
This will supercharge your vibration particularly when you get to a tricky part of the journey, or you are just feeling stuck.

The power of your energy is awesome and your Higher Self will ignite this anytime you ask. So ask away. You do

not have to struggle. Now that you are a conscious creator you get to decide how you want to feel. You get to decide it all. Feel the Joy just in this statement alone.
This is Emotional Freedom.
This is what Awakening is all about.

It is always possible to Choose Love, Live with Love and Flow with Love through each and every day.

As I am writing this right now I can feel the Love from Sarah, I can feel the Love from my Non-Physical team. I can feel my Love for me as I feel the Joy in what I have created. I have tears in my eyes and love in my heart and I am pocketing it all. I am setting Truths with my Higher Self along the way. I can feel them land solidly in my Truth vortex. I can feel the Truth of my Creation. I am showing my Soul to you all so you can feel the Truth in these words. So you can set the intention with your Higher Self to feel the Truth of you.

IT FEELS FLIPPING AWESOME!!

I am just going to sit and bathe in this energy they are igniting within me for a little while. I highly recommend you do this too when you feel the high vibration flow within you, as you can then expand it and use it over and over again.

Every action you are taking towards your Creation is strengthening your Knowing, we are all born with this capability, and it is in the exercising of it that will expand it for you.

Your Knowing helps you receive with more clarity from your Higher Self. Your Knowing builds confidence within you about your actions and decisions you make and it feels so empowering.

Your Knowing ignites the Trust in you and all you receive from your Higher Self and Non-Physical team.

Your Knowing will allow you to receive so much insight about your Soul Contract and the wondrous journey that awaits you. Yes there is so much more goodness waiting for you.

It is time now for each and every single human to take responsibility for their Life in a way that enables Emotional Freedom, Love and Hope.

It is time now to feel a deeper connection between you and the Universe.
It is time now for you to feel how important you are to the expansion of the Universe the multi-verse and Beyond.

It is time now for you to FEEL GOOD in all you Choose to do.
If your dream is sitting on the sofa with a bottle of wine binge watching Netflix if it FEELS GOOD do it.
If your dream is to relocate to another country to experience life in a different way, if it FEELS GOOD do it.
If your Dream is to have a new home with all the trimmings, if it FEELS GOOD do it.
If your Hope is to create a business that gives you financial freedom, if it FEELS GOOD do it.
If your Hope is that you can sell up, buy a camper van and travel to new places, if it FEELS GOOD do it.

If your dream is a job in a huge corporate business or working for a small independent business, if it FEELS GOOD do it.

If your Dream is to become an author, singer, artist, pub landlord, garden landscaper, builder, cleaner, police officer, pilot, designer, dancer, anything at all if it FEELS GOOD do it.

⋛ HOPES & DREAMS ⋛

Our point is that your Hopes and Dreams are unique and perfect for you, and therefore it is only you that should decide what that entails, and of course your Hopes and Dreams will not match those of others and that is perfectly perfect.

What is IMPORTANT is that all your Hopes and Dreams FEEL GOOD to YOU as and when you decide to do them.

Energy changes always, it is always in motion. Know that it is perfectly OK for your Hopes and Dreams to change as you change. Therefore your Desires may change too. This is OK. They should change as you change as we are here to experience as much of Life as we can in this one and only physical Life and therefore we will want to try out as many different experiences as we possibly can.

204

This is Your Life and you get to choose what it entails and how you ignite the Love within it. You know how to do this know in alignment with the Laws of the Universe. You know how to do this without fear holding you back. You know how good it feels to do exactly what lights up your Soul and puts the fire into your Desires.

Throughout the whole process find the Joy in all you do, look for it in the smallest of places and feel the gratitude within each joyful moment.

IF IT
FEELS
GOOD
do it

Joy is in All

*Joy in a positive comment that was
shared with you*

*Joy in the completion of an action
you have seen through*

*Joy in the confidence you are gaining
in all you do*

*Joy in the Fears you are re-labelling and detaching
from you*

Joy in the places you get to visit to be you

*Joy in the Nature that surrounds
and nurtures you*

Joy from a smile that does not know you

*Joy from the child that hugs you when
you are blue*

*Joy from the Sun that shines brightly
down on you*

*Joy from the Moon that lightens the
path ahead for you*

*Joy from the Love of the Universe
for all that you do*

*Joy from the expansion of your
Soul shinning through*

*Joy for each new day that allows you
to flow through*

*Joy from all the souls that are here
to support you*

*Joy from all you teach to others to align to the
Truth of You*

Joy from the laughter when something tickles you

Joy for each moment that allows you to be you

*Joy ignited with Love will always
see you through*

*~Karen, Sarah and Team~
January 2021*

≥ UNIVERSE DOWNLOAD ≤

≥ UNIVERSE DOWNLOAD ≤

CELEBRATE GOOD TIMES

Celebrate Good Times, Come On, It's a Celebration..

Oh I do Love that song and in case you had not noticed, music allows you and me to feel so so good. Sound holds an incredible vibration that your Soul recognises. That is the wondrous energy of Creation. It allows you to get into the zone. It brings you to a different plane; The Creativity plane is one place I go to when I am in the zone.

There is no better time to go there than now. We have been there many times together throughout this process. We went to the Creativity Plane to explore your possibilities. We went there to pull and Magnetise your Creation to you. We went there to Allow Focus. We went there to Ignite and Grow the Belief in your possibility and in you. We went to this wondrous plane to Harness the Creation energy and Wield it with your Soul. We went there Trigger possibilities into probabilities. We went there to Enact Change for you and your ability to ignite the Curiosity energy into your possibility.

The Creativity plane enabled the Spotlight energy to beam onto your Creation. We went to the Creativity Plane for many reasons throughout this process and at this stage it is not important to know it all but just know you can set the intention to go there when you Desire. Your Higher Self knows what to do. You just need to set the intention.

Of course you can go to this Plane and any other Plane for that matter when you choose to but today we are hanging out on the Creativity plane, because we are Celebrating Creation.

Celebrating your Creation, even if you are only just getting started with it, you are going to energise it through the wonderful high vibration energy of Celebration.

Energising the celebration of success through acknowledging every achievement you make. This exercises your Self Love. This expands the Trust in you. This expands your Self Worth. This strengthens your Love for You. You deserve to feel awesome. You are a Celebration of Life itself.

Allow yourself to submerge in the energy of Celebration.

Every time you take a step forward Celebrate
Every time you complete a task Celebrate.
Every time you understand something new Celebrate.
Every time you let go of low vibration Celebrate.
Every time you allow a new perspective Celebrate.
Every time you receive a compliment Celebrate.
Every time you see a change in you or those you are influencing Celebrate.
Every time you energise a positive change within Celebrate

Actually we are encouraging you to Celebrate every single aspect of your life as much as you can on a daily basis. Why?? Because this is an awesome high vibration energy that raises your transitional vibration and if you predominantly hold a high vibration during your day, when you sleep at night it will hold and store as high vibration and shift out the low stored vibration within you and then you will start to feel better in your Mind and Body thus aligning deeper with your Soul.

⸗ CELEBRATE ⸗

Each and every one of us Desire to 'Feel Good' on a daily basis. That is fundamentally our goal in life. We spend our life searching for what it is that will make us feel good and that is all part of the fun of living a physical life. Yet we hold the key within us always on how to 'Feel Good'. It is now high time we found happiness within us and then explored avenues of fun to expand it. It is time we took the lead role in our Life and played the game of Life as we choose to.

From a place of high Vibration and fully Love labelled when we try something new and it does not quite fit or align to our Soul we can let it go happily and move on to the next experience with Emotional Freedom.
Feel the power in living life this way. Feel the Truth that this is a Possibility for All who choose to Allow.

Exercising Celebration from the smallest of things like making a lovely cup of tea, doing the washing, having a catch up with your friends and family, to starting up your own business, completing a painting or even writing a book. No thing is exempt from celebration. It enhances the energy of Gratitude. You all know how powerful Gratitude can feel and that the more you feel Gratitude the more you get to feel Grateful for. You do not need to pop the cork for every celebration to feel its energy, you can Celebrate with a dance, a singsong, by congratulating yourself out loud, and there are many ways to generate the same energy without corks popping. But you know by now that I say if it 'Feels Good' do it!

Celebration energy hold's an even stronger energy when you combine it with Gratitude it lights up your Vortex of Emotions, Trust, Love, Hope, Truth and Strength and ignites Faith. The Faith in you, the Faith in God, the Faith in your Soul, the Faith in your journey and the Faith in Life itself.

The more you allow yourself to Celebrate the more ways to Celebrate will flow to you. Like attracts Like right? This energy is ignited within you it is where your Magic lives in your Soul.
Each and every single human holds Magic within their Soul makeup and it is just bursting to be let loose on this planet. It is bursting to co-create with you. You are a born creator and we are so so happy that you chose to be part of our Creation.

We will Celebrate completing this book, we will Celebrate every time someone chooses to purchase a book, we will Celebrate receiving messages from you about your wonderful Creations, and we will Celebrate seeing this book in publication. We will celebrate the holding of it physically. We will celebrate knowing we have shared our Love and Hope with you so that you too can start to feel as Happy and Loved as we do.

When I refer to 'We' I of course refer to my wonderful Higher Self Sarah and my incredible Non-Physical team that have shared this leading edge insight with me.
My family will no doubt Celebrate having a bit more of my attention.
Their support of course has been invaluable.

I feel a deep Gratitude of all I have gained through this process of Creation. I hold this wondrous energy for it all in my heart.

I feel a deep admiration for each and every person who allows himself or herself to embark on this wondrous journey of Awakening.

⇒ GOOD TIMES ⇐

My Hope is that you give yourself time to settle in every step. Allow yourself to settle in every achievement. Allow yourself to feel the excitement of the possibilities that are waiting for your energy to align to. There is always more to follow. It is the beautiful perpetual motion of life, the difference now is you are awake and ready to curate it your way.

There is no end to this exploration and discovery of life's potential Creations that await us this is what s so exciting about Curiosity and What If!
More importantly though, reflecting upon how this wondrous understanding can change the vibration of all for all.

Imagine incorporating into every aspect of your life this wondrous understanding of choosing Love over Fear.
Imagine if loved ones started living their life with this knowledge and how more understanding your family relationships would have within them.
Imagine if your colleagues at work lived their life with this knowledge and how the dynamics would change in the work place.
Imagine if your communities were all living consciously whole the incredible impact this would have on all within it.
You can see how this simple understanding and its powerful ripple effects will impact the vibration of our planet in time.

You are Ready now to explore further now with the perspective of Love Consciously Whole.

It is time now for all of you to 'Awaken Your Creation'

We love you xxx

Celebrate Gratitude

When you have the Attitude of Gratitude
You open up your heart to Love

When you have an Attitude of Gratitude
You are inviting Hope from above

When you have an Attitude of Gratitude
You can fill your heart with Joy

When you have an Attitude of Gratitude
You will receive Abundance to deploy

~Karen and Sarah~
March 2020

the truth is

YOU DESERVE LOVE

you deserve joy

YOU DESERVE HOPE

you deserve freedom

you
DESERVE ALL YOUR HOPES
& DREAMS IN ABUNDANCE

AWAKEN YOUR CREATION

218

Printed in Great Britain
by Amazon